Best regards,
Bruce T Blythe

BLINDSIDED

BLINDSIDED

A MANAGER'S GUIDE TO

CATASTROPHIC INCIDENTS

IN THE WORKPLACE

BRUCE T. BLYTHE

CEO
Crisis Management International, Inc.

PORTFOLIO

PORTFOLIO
Published by the Penguin Group
Penguin Putnam Inc., 375 Hudson Street, New York, New York 10014, U.S.A.
Penguin Books Ltd, 80 Strand, London WC2R 0RL, England
Penguin Books Australia Ltd, 250 Camberwell Road, Camberwell, Victoria 3124, Australia
Penguin Books Canada Ltd, 10 Alcorn Avenue, Toronto, Ontario, Canada M4V 3B2
Penguin Books India (P) Ltd, 11 Community Centre, Panchsheel Park,
New Delhi—110 017, India
Penguin Books (N.Z.) Ltd, Cnr Rosedale and Airborne Roads, Albany, Auckland, New Zealand
Penguin Books (South Africa) (Pty) Ltd, 24 Sturdee Avenue, Rosebank,
Johannesburg 2196, South Africa

Penguin Books Ltd, Registered Offices: Harmondsworth, Middlesex, England

First published in 2002 by Portfolio, a member of Penguin Putnam Inc.

1   3   5   7   9   10   8   6   4   2

PUBLISHER'S NOTE: This publication is designed to provide accurate
and authoritative information in regard to the subject matter covered. It is
sold with the understanding that the publisher is not engaged in rendering legal,
accounting or other professional services. If you require legal advice or other
expert assistance, you should seek the services of a competent professional.

LIBRARY OF CONGRESS CATALOGING IN PUBLICATION DATA
Blythe, Bruce T.
Blindsided : a manager's guide to catastrophic incidents in the workplace / Bruce T. Blythe.
p.   cm.
ISBN 1-59184-000-7
1. Violence in the workplace.   2. Emergency management.   3. Crisis management.
I. Title
HD5549.5.E43 B59   2002
658.4'056—dc21   2002070419

This book is printed on acid-free paper. ∞

Printed in the United States of America
Designed by Nancy Resnick

Page 235 is a continuation of this copyright page.

This book is dedicated to

Alex Gross

As a holocaust survivor against unbelievable odds, you have
demonstrated amazing resiliency, forgiveness, unselfish giving
and true enjoyment in humankind.

As a man whose wife was murdered, you have shown how love
can truly overshadow fear, depression and anger.

And as a parent who witnessed the accidental death of your
teenaged son, you have deeply touched countless thousands
of children in schools across the nation.

You give us all hope.

ACKNOWLEDGMENTS

No book, or career for that matter, can be successfully executed without the support of many people. I have been blessed with a truly wonderful support system. The worldwide network of professional consultants in our company is unsurpassed in their commitment to top quality services. The people we serve deserve no less than the best and I'm so proud to have you on our team. The corporate staff of Crisis Management International is the finest with whom I have ever worked. Mary Cardin, I couldn't have done it without your loyalty and management abilities. For the past sixteen years you have been the glue that has held us all together. Thanks to Linda Roach for attentive coordination of the manuscript. My gratitude also goes to Pamela Porter for her contributions to this book, and for all she does for CMI. And to Norm Shockley: Even in your retirement, your influence has supported untold thousands of people. Thanks for twelve solid years. Your professionalism and ethics continue to light CMI's path.

In writing this book, I had phenomenal support of the best, led by Robyn Freedman Spizman. Thank God for you, Robyn, and for your unwavering belief in me and this project. Evie Saks and Jonathan Lerner provided the support I needed every step of the way, and you know I couldn't have made it without you. A special thanks also to my literary agent, Meredith Bernstein, who made this book happen at lightning speed. And to Bill Brazell and Adrian Zackheim for believing in this book and making it a reality.

So many corporate folks have stood out over the years and contributed to my knowledge of crisis management. Thanks especially to the Kerr-McGee corporate team of Tom Knight, John Reichenberger, Pete Woodward and Ken Crouch. You guys set the best practice standards in crisis preparedness.

James Kreindler, thanks for your input on Pan Am 103. Charlie McDonald, you are the "real thing" in simulations. An additional thanks to Jack Cox of Liberty Mutual, Chris Nelson of Target Corporation and Joy Sever of the Reputation Institute for their valuable assistance. Gene Rugala, thanks for sharing the knowledge of the FBI Academy and for your friendship.

I want to acknowledge my wife, Becky, and my daughter, Alexandria. You two have given me the space to pursue my dreams and I love both of you beyond words. And I don't want to forget Clue, our dog who insisted that we continue to run around the neighborhood while the book writing was taking place.

I also want to recognize all those individuals who have been subjected to traumatic incidents throughout my career. We have learned much together along the way. And I want to pay tribute to all those unsuspecting people who will be subjected to catastrophes in the future. Hopefully, the contents of this book will reach you and be helpful during your time of great need.

Last of all, I want to acknowledge you, the reader. If even one catastrophe is avoided, or the well-being of only a single person is protected, the value of the information in this book is priceless.

CONTENTS

FOREWORD

When the Murrah Federal Building in Oklahoma City exploded on April 19, 1995, I was less than two blocks away in our corporate headquarters. The shock wave blew out some one hundred windows in the Kerr-McGee Tower, causing many of my colleagues to believe that it was our building that had been bombed.

Fortunately, we had prepared. But when Kerr-McGee Corporation, an $11 billion oil, gas and chemical company, first enlisted the services of Bruce Blythe and Crisis Management International, we certainly never dreamed that such a horrific act of terrorism would take place right in our own neighborhood.

Emerging elements of the modern world can threaten any organization. Yet with proper preparation and guidance from crisis management professionals, I now know that you can influence the effects that catastrophes have on your organization.

This is not to say that our people are no longer affected by the OKC bombing. None of us will forget that tragic day. But I can personally attest to the crisis management system outlined in this book. With it, we managed to work through this crisis together. Now we are a stronger, more compassionate organization.

No one can predict the site of the next catastrophe, but all of us can—and must—prepare for the possibility that it will hit our neighborhood.

During the past thirty years, 80 percent of terrorist attacks on American targets have been directed at corporations. In its continually evolving forms, terrorism has become one more risk for all companies to face—along with workplace violence, industrial accidents, product tampering and natural disasters.

We use the crisis preparedness services of Crisis Management International throughout our corporation—in the U.S., Europe, China and Australia. In all of our locations, CMI set up a humanitarian response program to supplement our emergency response capabilities. As CEO of a *Fortune* 500 company, I appreciate the importance of addressing the needs of the business and our valued shareholders. We can address those needs only by making a sincere effort to attend to our people, who are truly our most valuable asset.

Bruce Blythe has distilled his knowledge into a book that is powerful, accessible and complete. It will help you lead your organization through disaster—mostly by helping you prepare for it.

The goal of crisis management is for your organization to survive. You may never get back to exactly where you were before. But a well-managed crisis can actually leave your organization stronger, more resilient and better tuned to the world than it was before.

The need to prepare your company for crisis has never been so clear. The guidance you need is in this book.

Luke R. Corbett
Chairman and Chief Executive Officer
Kerr-McGee Corporation

INTRODUCTION

Terrorism. Earthquakes. Hostage situations. As the CEO of Crisis Management International, an Atlanta-based crisis consulting firm with clients around the world, I have dealt with countless earth-shattering events. The impossible-to-imagine tragedies that are the stuff of "Breaking News" fill my average workday.

I have witnessed the life-changing events that rock our world.

To save kidnap and ransom hostages, I have trekked deep into the jungle of Ecuador.

I was at a school bus crash in Texas that resulted in the tragic loss of twenty-three young children.

In the aftermath of Hurricane Andrew, my firm provided relief to twenty-eight companies simultaneously.

And then, on July 29, 1999, it was our turn. A crazed gunman was on the loose in the office complex that is home to our company, Crisis Management International (CMI). As I walked to our front door to assure it was locked, I was informed by my office manager that our vice president of Operations, a trusted and loyal employee of sixteen years, had just left for the bank through the very corridor where the gunman reportedly was on the loose.

I was overcome with an immediate need to rush out to assist. Yet my years of crisis experience training told me this was a time to put my veteran crisis management team and our communications capabilities into action.

The shooter, we would come to learn, was Mark Barton, a disgruntled day-trader in Atlanta's financial district. By day's end he would kill nine people and injure another dozen. My immediate concern was for our vice president. The question I presented to our staff was, *"Now what do we do?"*

I reached for the crisis manual, the same one that has evolved through use with countless CMI clients over the years. It was our turn to take our own medicine. The Checklist for Immediate Actions reminded us to address ongoing danger, communications with those impacted, notifications, family concerns and escalation potential.

Before long, we were told erroneously that the gunman was holed up in an office *in our building* with hostages. We were instructed to stay away from windows and hallways. Through the plate glass front window, I could see police officers running with guns drawn. Something big was going down and this time our role was potential target, not crisis management consultants. Eerily, our staff watched on television as our building appeared on the screen.

Finally, we received the phone call we had been waiting for, but dreading. It was good news—our vice president was unhurt! In fact, she had been the second person on the scene and had been pressed into service to tend to frightened employees in other offices. Two hours later, police officers finally escorted us from the building. Our staff members recoiled as we were led past the nearby office whose glass walls revealed a sickening saga of death and destruction.

After years of helping others cope with traumatic incidents, this experience gave me and my colleagues at CMI a new perspective on experiencing crisis. We were near the shooting and identified closely with the incident. The impact on all of us was considerable.

Although begun before the attacks of September 11, 2001, this book was completed with recognition that the rules have changed. A sense of safety and security once commonplace among employees and employers has been severely compromised. The possibilities for crisis in the workplace are more ominous and far more real.

The events of September 11th succeeded in heightening the awareness of business leaders that anything, and everything is now possible. They see—as they have never seen before—that *strong, proactive measures are required to protect their workers and, in turn, their businesses and reputations.*

My goal in writing *Blindsided* was to bring order and purpose to the potentially overwhelming task of preparing for crisis. I want to help reduce your company's exposure to chaos and threat, by teaching you to analyze foreseeable risks and create a master plan for crisis response. These are lessons that until recently may have seemed merely interesting. Now they have become essential.

I bring my years of experience to these pages. The middle-of-the-night calls from frantic executives. The heartrending visits to hospitals. And the palpable desolation as colleagues gather around a television, learning that the hijacking victim on the screen is one of their own.

The first half of this book covers field-tested approaches for responding to critical incidents *during the heat of battle.* The second half offers a structured methodology for preparing your organization for crisis, in advance. It is intended to be used at a slower pace, as you plan and enhance your crisis preparedness over time.

I placed the section on response before that on preparedness to give a full understanding of what you will encounter in a real disaster, before you start to develop a plan. To prepare adequately for crisis, you need to "see" what you are up against.

Each chapter is followed by a Quick Use Guide, a tool for instant reference during a crisis or any time. The final chapter provides additional checklists, guidelines and management considerations for a range of specific crises, from natural disasters and workplace murders, to corporate kidnappings and air crashes.

My message offers unparalleled relevance to today's workplace. But these are not newly minted, untried concepts. Rather, these are lessons I have learned and shared with business leaders around the world for two decades.

CMI's ideas and strategies have been put to use by leading corporations that range from medium-sized companies to a Who's Who of the *Fortune* 500. These methods have helped forward-thinking managers respond to those terrible events that no one wants to anticipate—but that no one can afford any longer to pretend will not occur.

I saw them work in the rubble of the September 11th attacks. Amid chaos, death and unspeakable destruction, well-trained, prepared companies were able to quickly react, assessing the needs of their people and putting into place the plans they never wanted to need. And they will work for you.

I have witnessed the devastation that can result when unprepared managers are left to respond through improvisation. Conversely, I have seen the overwhelmingly centered, positive results when employers reach out with appropriate communications and actions to manage not only the physical, but the emotional after effects of a crisis.

Yesterday's crisis management plan does not accommodate the possibilities of tomorrow. What's needed by businesses now is a proven method to assure that not only your facilities are rebuilt, but that the spirit, cohesion and productivity of your employees are, too.

It is my hope that the ideas and instruction contained in these pages will be thoroughly understood and practiced—and hopefully never put to the real test. But if you follow them and crisis does strike, you will be ready. You may feel concerned and unsure in some ways, but *you will not be blindsided.* It is my pleasure to assist you as you strive to achieve the calm assurance of preparedness.

Bruce T. Blythe
CEO
Crisis Management International, Inc.
Atlanta, Georgia

BLINDSIDED

PART 1

RESPONSE

CHAPTER 1

Now What Do You Do?
Immediate Aftermath Phase

It is a normal Thursday morning—except that because it's raining, you had to drop the kids at school, so you got to your desk late. Fourteen of your sixty-six e-mails are flagged "priority," there are twelve voice mails—and you have to make a presentation to the top brass at 10:30. You are just settling in to go over your notes, when there is a short burst of dull pops.

So short and dull, that until you hear the screaming, you don't actually register the sounds.

But you hear the second burst with heart-stopping clarity, and the third—and the shattering of plate glass, and the panicked screaming, and the commotion of chairs being kicked over and doors slammed, as people stumble for cover from the gunman who is terrorizing the place you work.

Your instinct is to scream and hide, too—except that you are the person who has been designated to manage crisis response.

Here Are Tools You Can Respond With

In this book, I will share experiences, tools and techniques to help assure that you and your employees avoid being blindsided by a catastrophic incident. They're the same field-tested strategies and tactics that we utilize with our clients, who include some of the best known companies and governmental organizations in the world.

Throughout the book, I will keep it simple, offering concrete, take-and-use guidelines to help you improve your crisis IQ and skill base. The book is divided into two sections—crisis response and crisis preparedness.

The first section provides strategies and tactics for responding in the aftermath of a catastrophic incident. While it assumes a "big one," the tools it gives you will work just as well to help you keep smaller crises well in hand. The second, preparedness section will show you that *there is little possibility of effective response without thoughtful preparedness.* It will lead you through the steps you need to take toward preparedness, before another disaster strikes your organization.

Imagining the Worst, and Picturing What to Do

The mental tool of *focused imagery* can help you be more effective as a crisis manager.

It's hard to imagine your company, let alone yourself, in the throes of a disaster or traumatic incident. Typically, when we confront the idea of trauma, our minds dissociate or block it out. In many ways, that is a healthy response. It keeps us from being chronically anxiety ridden. But it can also prevent us from concentrating productively, as we should, on harmful possibilities. In the chapters on preparedness, I will show you how to use focused imagery exercises to make sure that your crisis planning is thorough and relevant to the real risks you face.

Imagery can also help you make it through a "live" crisis. While consulting at crisis sites, I often imagine myself in the place of those involved. For example, to help craft the key messages that management should communicate to the media, I imagine myself as an aggressive reporter. What information would help me tell the most riveting story? What spin might I be tempted to put on the story as a result of past coverage or the company's image in the community? What evidence of controversy or negligence might I look for to attract attention? After doing this, I find myself able, with surprising accuracy, to anticipate the questions the media will throw at us, and the spin they might be put on the incident.

This imagery technique will help you recognize what's needed, and will accelerate your response time—when there's no time to lose.

It's Happening Right Here, and Right Now—to Us

If a shooting occurred at your place of work, what would your employees need from you, the crisis manager? Put yourself in the place of any typical employee, and apply the focused imagery technique to our hypothetical situation of the rampaging gunman.

Impact phase. Imagine that you are working at your desk. Suddenly, you hear shots, breaking glass and screaming. The first spray of gunfire was at a location you could not see, but now the shooter comes running up the hallway, toward and then past your office—stopping to blast into a few open doorways, terrifyingly, seemingly at random—as he heads for an exit.

While it may be uncomfortable, you should imagine as vividly as possible the shocking sounds, the sickening sights, the rush of adrenaline and pounding of your heart, even the burnt metallic scent of the gunpowder.

What would be your immediate reactions? If you are like most of us, your reaction would be focused on survival. Your response would be to run, hide or play dead, or possibly to attack the gunman if you were close enough and it appeared to be your best option for survival. *Flee, freeze or fight.* Now what?

Immediately afterward. Assume you and others have rapidly evacuated the building to a nearby sidewalk. Fellow employees are standing around, shell-shocked and stressed. Everybody feels physically bedraggled, too. Adrenaline is flowing. Some are in tears.

Envision the reactions you would have at this point, five minutes to an hour following the incident. What might you imagine feeling? Your sense of safety, security and control are shattered. There is fear that the shootings may not be over. You feel exposed. You are shocked, stunned and dazed. The need for information is tremendous—questions abound and answers are few in the *immediate aftermath* phase. It seems unreal, almost like a dream that you are observing. The incident is too shocking and big for your mind to adequately grasp. You have multiple feelings—yet you feel numb, too.

Hours later. Continuing the imagery, you've returned home after giving a statement to the police and being released by your superiors. As you sink into a comfortable chair or huddle over tea at the kitchen table, the enormity of the day's events starts to hit you with a vengeance.

Adrenaline courses through your body throughout the rest of the day and into the evening. There is a continuing need for information—some of which may come eerily to you over the media, or through calls from family members, friends or colleagues.

Before long, the phone intrusions will begin to feel overwhelming and you may withdraw from further contact. Stress and exhaustion struggle for supremacy, but you are wired, unable to rest. You refuse food, perhaps indulging in a stiff drink over anything more wholesome. Denial and the reality of the experience hit your mind in waves, called numbing and flooding.

By bedtime, you are strangely exhausted physically and emotionally, but not sleepy. As your head hits the pillow, flashbacks from the day's events spill into your mind, colliding crazily. You want to rewind the experience as if it hadn't happened at all, or had been nothing more than a nasty nightmare. You start to second guess yourself in other ways and, although you know it's pointless, can't stop. The "what ifs" and "if onlys" are dragging you to places you don't want to be.

"What if I had been one of those he shot?" "If I had rushed him, could I have saved people?" "What would my family be experiencing now, if I had been killed?" "What are the families of those who were shot going through now?"

Sleep seems impossible. As the hours tick by, guilt begins to push through the cracks of your fragmented soul. Anger takes up residence as well. Anxiety reactions are as likely as the sunrise. Flashbacks, intrusive thoughts and concentration difficulties abound.

The aftermath phase. Now you find yourself in the *aftermath phase.* After a sleepless, despondent night, you have been asked to return to the workplace the next day. You comb the newspaper to gain needed information. Without breakfast (your stomach continues to revolt), you begin the physical and emotional journey back to the site of the shooting.

How do you feel as you arrive on the property? What might you experience as you walk into the building? Feelings of anxiety, maybe even panic, are likely, though you attempt to put on your best face. Some coworkers are busying themselves at their workstations; others seem dazed and barely able to function.

Nobody, it seems, looks as bad as you feel. You begin to ask yourself,

"Have I lost it?" "Am I going crazy?" Despite the lack of sleep, you feel surprisingly awake. But the idea that you might have to fully apply yourself to work tasks seems almost a joke—there is absolutely no way you could do it. **As an employee in the aftermath, what do you really need?** Now, ask yourself. What do you need from management, as you arrive back at work for the first time following the horrible tragedy?

You and your coworkers will want evidence that you are safe, with visibly increased physical security. Management needs to show overt signs of compassion and caring. You need accurate and timely information. You want some understanding regarding your inability to work at a 100-percent productivity level, no matter how pressing work demands may be.

Full concentration on work is simply beyond your mental, emotional and physical capabilities right now. You may or may not want to see the scene where the incident occurred. You want answers as to why it occurred and what could have been done to prevent the incident. You want acceptable evidence that management is doing everything humanly possible to prevent this kind of thing from ever happening again.

If you are your organization's crisis manager, once you go through this focused imagery exercise, the needs of your employees no longer seem vague. You can begin to see the concrete things you should do to protect and support them.

Focused imagery can be used with any affected group or individual. What if you were a member of the company's board of directors? What if you were an employee of the company in another city? Or the spouse of a casualty, a reporter, an Emergency Medical Technician, a customer or a stockholder. Your crisis management effectiveness will soar when you move from an arm's length, detached perspective to an intimately imagined understanding of all these various experiences. And when you do this exercise, don't neglect to imagine your own experience.

Managing Your Way Through a Crisis

Let's go through the exercise again, using the same workplace shooting incident. Only this time, the experience you imagine will be your own, as the company's crisis manager.

Impact phase. Like everyone else, you experience the natural human impulses of fear, flight or fight. But you know your obligation is to spring into action. Through an act of sheer conscious will, you catch your breath, focus on the situation before you, and start working. You may find yourself running against the stream. As others are running out, you are running to the scene or to your pre-designated Crisis Command Center to take your initial response actions.

Immediately afterward. What must you do first? The tasks seem too numerous, and overwhelming, but you discipline your mind to put them in a logical order. Verify that adequate police and emergency medical help have been summoned. See that everyone who was not injured is evacuated to a safe place. Try to determine where the shooter has gone, if he remains a threat—and who he might have been. Secure those areas where shooting occurred.

Hours later. The police and ambulances arrive, followed almost immediately by the television vans. The police cordon off the building, and determine that the gunman has left the vicinity. After taking statements from the uninjured employees, they are ready to release them. It seems, from these statements, that the shooter was a former employee who was laid off in a recent downsizing. The police need someone from Human Resources to give them details that could help track him down.

Meanwhile, the employees are distraught at the idea of leaving on their own, and confused about whether they should come to work tomorrow. You need to address their concerns and help get them off the premises. That's going to involve protecting them from the pack of reporters lining the driveway. You need to assure them they have no obligation to talk, and that a company spokesperson will handle the press.

The first "breaking news" alerts have brought many employees' family members to the site, desperate to know if their loved ones were among the injured or killed. You will need to delegate someone to receive them, take them someplace protected, tell them what happened and connect them with their loved ones.

The aftermath phase. The suspected shooter, your former employee, has been arrested at his home. So presumably there's no more actual danger. But uncomfortable questions are already being asked about his tenure at the company, why and how he was let go, and whether you could have realized that he posed a danger. You need to develop a coherent message about this incident, for dissemination both to the outside world and internally. Customers, suppliers, members of your board, and others are all clamoring to know what happened, what you expect to come of it and how it is being handled.

Your people will be coming back in the morning. How will you welcome them, and help them work through the trauma? You need to plan meetings, debriefings and onsite treatment for them. Perhaps the scene of the shooting should be preserved long enough for any who want to revisit it.

You're exhausted. And there's still so much to do. But things have begun to calm down, and a question occurs to you: How are you managing? How are those you're delegating to functioning? As things begin to settle down, you realize that observing and tracking your response, and noting the things you wish you'd had in place, will be invaluable for future crisis planning, and you make some notes.

Programming Your Brain for Effectiveness

As a crisis manager you can program your brain through focused imagery, simulations and training. It's the same mentality used in military training, simulation training for commercial airline pilots, and the teaching of martial arts. The learned, exercised response becomes routine, even in an emergency.

Preparation will leave you less bewildered and your employees more secure in your ability to safeguard them in time of need. It's like an insurance policy that you would never consider canceling. Planning, training, rehearsing and visualizing provide your brain pathways with a system that can be activated smoothly and efficiently when the time comes.

But what if the crisis is happening right now, and preparedness is something you have not adequately done?

In the next nine chapters I will lead you through the essential steps of any crisis response, starting with initial notification. My message in Chapter Two is strong and simple: The way you receive information and respond can have an incredibly strong impact on the ultimate outcome of the crisis.

Quick Use Response Guide

CHAPTER 1: *NOW* WHAT DO YOU DO?

IMMEDIATE AFTERMATH PHASE

- While it may feel uncomfortable, open your mind to the imagined horror and aftermath of a catastrophe long enough to adequately plan out, *"Now what do I do?"* for each affected audience.
- Refer to the Quick Use Response Guides that follow each of the next nine chapters for specific, point-by-point help in crafting your response.

CHAPTER 2

Receiving Initial Notification

It's one of those things you never forget—the precise moment in time when you learned some dreadful piece of news. Like the death of a loved one, the assassination of a political figure or a fatal accident where you live or work.

You can probably remember the period following that call quite vividly. Time may have slowed eerily. Thoughts and movements thickened. You felt dread and fear—a nauseating feeling that grips you and won't let go.

Even when the context is professional, the reaction is personal. As a manager confronted with a fire that's consumed your workplace and threatened your staff, the sickening sensations are the same as those experienced by someone who learns a personal tragedy has occurred.

Three Ways to Get the News

Notification of a catastrophe at your place of business can take one of three forms. You may be personally involved in the incident, and a firsthand observer. In this case, your initial perceptions and responses will be inevitably altered by the fact that you will be shocked, stunned and dazed, like everyone else involved. But you'll have to take steps to overcome those sensations more quickly than others, because you must manage this unfolding horror.

In the second scenario, you may be near the incident scene, but not directly involved—in another part of the building, perhaps.

In both the first and second scenarios, despite your proximity to the events, accurate information is difficult to obtain. Rumors bubble up quickly. A true and accurate fact pattern has not yet emerged. One company that we work with has a sign in their Crisis Command Center that states, "The initial facts coming in are mostly false."

The third possibility is that you will be remote from the incident. Here, the difficult challenge is to obtain accurate information from someone who is likely experiencing traumatic stress, even as you are coping with your own strong emotional reaction.

None of these scenarios is "easier" or more ideal than the others. In each case, you are likely dealing with partial information that carries overwhelming emotional weight. We all have varying abilities to cope with such stress—and of course, some do it better than others.

Breaking It Down

When an event occurs that pushes us beyond our normal coping mechanisms, we enter an emotional and cognitive zone that is out of the ordinary. A near-automatic reaction is to dissociate or push back the information, symbolized by the "Oh no!" reaction common among those who take in bad news. It's that feeling that the mind and body have become temporarily disconnected—a psychic and physical numbness.

Think about the experience of eating an apple. The only way it can be ingested is in bite-size pieces. Learning of a tragic event that affects people we know well is like asking the mind to gulp in an entire apple. The shock and sense of unreality are the mind's way of letting you know it can't cope with this giant intrusion.

You can process the information, but in "bite-size" pieces. Those pieces come in many forms, and over time. They include the flashbacks, concentration difficulties, intrusive thoughts and sleeplessness that many survivors of a catastrophe experience. But as a crisis response manager in the immediate impact phase of a disaster, you will have to concentrate all your mental energy on examining and "ingesting" all the fragments of information that come your way.

You'll Need to Act Fast

Picture yourself as a corporate crisis manager in the office where a shooting like the one I described in Chapter One has taken place. Without warning, gunfire and screams shatter the office's morning calm. Windows shatter, doors slam, furniture is knocked around, people rush by in the hallway. You hear the shouts: "Nancy's been shot! Oh, God, Jorge is dead!" Shots and screams are heard from several locations in the building, and someone yells, "There are people with guns!" You see one man, with a gun, run past your office, and down an exit stairway that leads to the back. The head of building security orders an evacuation, out the front doors.

Your initial notification was the sound of gunshots and screams, which "informed" you that something awful was happening. You saw one shooter reach the exit. But you distinctly heard someone yelling about "people with guns." Meanwhile, the employees are now congregating in the front courtyard. Should that decision be reconsidered? If a second gunman is still in the building, aren't they vulnerable there to his sniping? You locate the head of building security, explain your worry, and together decide to move the group into the parking deck. Within half an hour, police and security staff have searched the entire building and found no one.

The erroneous impression, part of your initial notification, that there was more than one perpetrator caused you to move an already traumatized group of people a second time, and have them wait in the less than comforting environment of the parking deck. Additionally, the lone gunman is now verified to be somewhere outside the building. Now you need to rescind the order to evacuate, and bring people back inside to a place where they and their immediate emotional needs can be comfortably addressed. This is not to suggest the order to move them to the parking deck was incorrect, based on the information at hand. It's just that the initial information at hand was wrong. The point: Initial information typically includes erroneous assumptions and misinformation. You may need to revise your first response at a moment's notice.

The Hunt for Information

The search for credible information is the first action step you take after notification of a catastrophe. There are four primary questions that, if asked and answered efficiently, will yield the essence of the information you need to strategize and implement your response.

- What happened?
- How bad is it?
- What is being done?
- What is the potential for escalation?

These questions appear straightforward, but on closer reflection each is surprisingly multifaceted. It is important to know what questions to ask. The information source may be frantic, injured or downright confused. It's your job to extract the most important information as quickly and accurately as possible.

Let's examine them individually in some detail.

Question #1: What Happened?!

Some points to consider as you seek to learn what has occurred:

If you're getting firsthand information, determine if the source has actually witnessed the events. That is the difference between *verified* and *unsubstantiated* firsthand accounting. Even with a firsthand accounting, there can be misperceptions and misinformation. A second accounting from another person might be in order, as time will allow.

If you're getting secondhand information, find out who told your source. How did he or she know it is accurate? Did that person who told your informant actually see it, or has the information been passed down the line?

If the information has not been verified, what steps need to be taken while verification is taking place? This could include dispatching of emergency vehicles, making internal notification, planning a statement to the media, referring to your crisis manual, alerting your Crisis Management Team and strategizing the details of your immediate response, should the incident be verified.

Make Every Minute Count

Have your prepared crisis manual and checklists ready so that you can act immediately upon verification. This is much easier if you have sufficient copies of your crisis manual stored at various locations, including at the office, at home and in the car. CMI recommends keeping copies both on your electronic handheld organizers and in your computer system. Be certain you can put your hands on it within minutes no matter where you are—even while traveling.

In the absence of a crisis manual, use the Quick Use Guide at end of Chapters One through Ten in the response section of this book.

Question #2: How Bad *Is* It?

As you take in information, your goal is to envision the scene as clearly as possible. Here again, visualization is an effective technique. Ask your informant, *"Describe what you see or know in as much detail as possible."* Have the informant describe the location and disposition of employees, the status of damaged buildings or equipment, etc. The more vivid the word picture, the better sense you can gain of the situation's severity and the steps that must be taken to create order out of chaos.

Be careful not to spend too much time gathering initial information. You want to balance getting adequate information with taking necessary immediate response actions. Use a subset of questions to assess severity:

PEOPLE

- Is there ongoing danger? Of what?
- What is the number of serious injuries and/or deaths? Are these confirmed?

- How many people are directly involved?
  - ○ Survivors actually present when the incident occurred
  - ○ Those who felt life-threatened
- How many may be indirectly involved?
  - ○ People with ties to the organization, location or your people
  - ○ People in the wider community

PROPERTY

- Has company property been damaged? How?
- Is the damage ongoing?

BUSINESS DISRUPTION

- Are operations continuing at full/normal levels, partial levels or stopped altogether?

SURROUNDINGS

- How widespread is the damage?
- How has the community been affected?
- Are there threats to or effects on surrounding property?

LIABILITY AND REPUTATION

Sometimes the cause of an accident can be more damaging than the incident itself. The media, regulators, competitors and others may be eager to affix blame following a severe incident. Learn the following:

- Are we at fault, or perceived to be at fault?
- In what ways may we be blamed?
- Is there any apparent outrage directed toward the organization, individual employees or management?
- What spin is the media putting on the story, if any, at this point?

Question #3: What Is Being Done?

The idea here is to get as accurate a picture as possible of the actions already being taken by on-site personnel and others. Again, think—and ask—in terms of people, property, business disruption and surroundings.

PEOPLE

- Is first aid being administered effectively? If necessary, give coaching or summon assistance.
- Have a sufficient number of emergency vehicles been dispatched? Can this information be verified?
- Are driveways accessible to emergency vehicles?
- Are employees, vendors, visitors and others out of harm's way?
- Are employees being protected from distressing sights and media encroachment?
- Have accommodations been made for family members who may call or arrive at the site?
- Are members of the media being accommodated, yet restrained from excessive intrusion?

PROPERTY

- What is being done to contain any continuing damage?
- Is the incident site being protected for investigation?
- How is the perimeter around the incident site being secured?
- How is the perimeter around the entire facility being secured?

BUSINESS DISRUPTION

- Should production be reduced or halted?
- Can employees remain at the work site safely?

- Should any areas of the facility be shut down? If not, do they need special attention to assure that they are secure?

SURROUNDINGS

- Are neighboring businesses/residents aware of the incident?
- Is there a need to notify them?

Question #4: What Is the Potential for Escalation?

The last of the four key questions is surely one of the most important. You need to know how the situation might escalate in severity and what can be done to avoid a worsening of conditions. The difference between a well-managed traumatic event and a situation spun out of control is often a crisis manager's ability to understand the potential for escalation and take steps to mitigate against it.

Be sure to ask:

- How could this situation or the aftereffects spin out of control?
- What controls need to be put in place to avoid escalation?
- What is being done to contain the causes and effects of the incident?

KEEP THE BIG PICTURE IN MIND

Take periodic time-outs to reflect quickly but effectively on your purpose and goals. Process those "bite-size" pieces of information. Ask questions like these:

- What are the priorities that need to be considered this hour and this day? What most urgently needs to be addressed in order to contain the crisis and, for example, ensure the safety of survivors, prevent any ongoing danger or physical damages, begin crisis communications, and the like.

- What are the biggest problems we face? Are they primarily, for example, business disruption, or traumatized people, or blame toward the company, or mounting financial losses, or a compromised reputation.
- What activities should be going on at the same time initial notification is taking place?
- Where is this incident headed?

The Balancing Act

Avoid the tendency to spend too much time assessing the situation; the goal is to get sufficient information to move forward with action steps and decisions.

Consider the following example. I was on the phone with a site manager who was in his car on a cell phone immediately following a workplace shooting. Police who were searching the area for the gunman had evacuated the site manager and all employees from the building.

As I was getting initial details from this manager, it became apparent that there were a number of employees standing near the building where the gunman was still on the loose. They had not yet been moved by police. Here is the conversation that took place:

BLYTHE: "How many of your people do you see standing around near the entrance?"

MANAGER: "About one hundred or more."

BLYTHE: "Is there an alternative place where they can immediately congregate?"

MANAGER: "Yes, we have a medical building across the property—it's about fifty yards away and it has a couple of large training rooms."

BLYTHE: "Do you see anyone nearby who can help you mobilize people and get them safely over there?"

MANAGER: "Yes, one of our people is standing near my vehicle."

BLYTHE: "Ask him to come over and tell him to enlist others to move everyone to the medical building immediately. Do it now while I wait on the phone."

Clearly, all the information needed had not yet been obtained, but immediate action had to be taken. After that action step was completed, the manager continued to brief me as completely as he could on the facts as he knew them. We felt much better knowing that dozens of employees were out of harm's way.

Initial notification is an extremely important process. In this chapter we covered issues including the four primary questions that must be asked and answered and the need to balance information-gathering with taking action.

In Chapter Three, the focus is on action steps—using the information you've received from the initial notification to start the process of making order out of chaos.

Quick Use Response Guide

CHAPTER 2: RECEIVING INITIAL NOTIFICATION

❑ What Happened?
  ✓ Incident described, verify accuracy of information.
    • Firsthand: Has notifier seen it with his/her own eyes?
    • Secondhand: Who told notifier? How do you know the information is accurate?
    • Not verified: What needs to be done while verification is being confirmed?

❑ How Bad Is It?
  ✓ People
    • Ongoing danger?
    • Number of serious injuries and deaths? How confirmed?
    • Number of emotionally traumatized individuals?
    • How may people are involved directly?
    • How many are indirectly involved, but affected?
  ✓ Property
    • What damages to company property?
    • Is the damage ongoing?
  ✓ Business disruption
    • Operation continuing at full/normal levels, partial levels or stopped?

✓ Surroundings
  • How widespread are the damages?
  • How has the community been affected?
  • Threats and effects on surrounding area?
✓ Liability/reputation
  • Are we at fault or perceived to be at fault?
  • In what ways are we being blamed?
  • Any apparent outrage?
  • To what extent is media involved?
  • What spin could media put on the story?

❑ What Is Being Done?
  ✓ People
    • Is first aid being administered effectively? By whom? Do they need relief?
    • Coach first-aid procedures, or summon assistance if needed.
    • Have sufficient emergency vehicles been dispatched?
    • Are driveways accessible to permit emergency vehicles to enter?
    • Are individuals out of harm's way?
    • Have people been evacuated or separated from danger?
    • What is being done for the injured?
    • What is being done with bodies of fatalities?
    • Which hospitals are utilized?
    • What is being done to protect onlookers from distressing sights?
    • Accommodations for family members who may arrive at the site?
    • What is being done to accommodate and restrict media representatives?
    • Is everyone accounted for?
  ✓ Property
    • What is being done to contain continuing property damage?
    • What is the plan to secure the perimeter around the incident site and company site?
    • Is the incident site secured to protect investigation?
  ✓ Business production
    • Should production be reduced or halted?
    • Can employees remain at the work site safely?
    • Should any area of the facility be shut down, or require special attention to assure security?

✓ Surroundings
  • Are others in the surrounding area aware of the incident?
  • Is there a need to notify others?

❏ Escalation Potential?
  • How could the effects of this situation escalate in severity?
  • What controls need to be put in place to avoid escalation?
  • What is being done to contain the causes and effects of the incident?

CHAPTER 3

Immediate Actions, Initial Response Phase

Your *initial response* at the time of a workplace trauma or catastrophic event can mean the difference between life and death, to people and to your organization. Your actions in those first minutes can help turn chaos into ultimate order. Or, the chaos can compound, spinning irretrievably out of control.

In this chapter, we will discuss:

- Five personal traits to demonstrate during this initial response phase.
- General guidelines when taking immediate actions.
- How to prioritize in the chaos of the early aftermath.
- Ten considerations for immediate actions.

A Manager in Crisis

Let's put you back in the immediate aftermath, but this time through another perspective. In Chapter One you visualized a workplace shooting from the viewpoint of an employee who was in the room at the time the gunman entered. In Chapter Two, you visualized yourself, a crisis manager working at your desk when the shootings took place. Let's pick up on that same situation, and examine what your initial responses might be.

You're at your desk when you hear shots and commotion. You hear screams, including someone yelling, "There are people with guns!" A lone Caucasian man in a red shirt runs by your door; you see him duck down an exit stairway that leads to the back.

You run spontaneously to the conference area on your floor, where shootings occurred, without any sense of potential exposure to personal danger. As you arrive, you see shell-shocked employees frantically attempting to administer first aid to victims lying in pools of blood. Tables and chairs are overturned and the smell of gun smoke is pungent in the air. Things look the same in the conference room, where people were also shot. Adrenaline is flowing.

You observe through the windows that employees are pouring out of the building into the forecourt. Back in the conference room, one manager lies gravely wounded and she appears dead. You are stunned. Others are down and appear seriously injured as well. Now you hear sirens outside the building. As you look out, you see the first police car arrive. Also, a television van and crew are pulling up to the front entrance. As the crisis manager, what are your immediate steps?

Let's take a look at issues that need management attention, based on what we already know.

We know there is a gunman on the loose, but we don't know where he is—or whether he was alone. Employees are outside the building, potentially exposed to the gunman—and now to the police, who don't yet know whom they are looking for. Several of your people are gravely injured, in need of prompt treatment. Media representatives have arrived and you are about to become the lead story.

Damage Control

A number of immediate steps must be taken. Among the most critical are the following:

Minimize ongoing danger. Employees are at risk since we don't know where the gunman is located, or if there was more than one. Quickly delegate some employees to direct others into a secured area, like a cafeteria. Assign another employee to assure the cafeteria is safe. Have the employee establish monitors at the doors to assure that only company personnel get in.

Help locate the gunman. The police need a description of the perpetrator. Your sighting of a Caucasian man in a red shirt who has allegedly run out of the building is corroborated by other witnesses—and nobody claims to have seen a second shooter. Have someone inform the police now, even though the information may not be complete. What you know can help.

Begin to address emergency medical needs. If there are known personnel who are trained in first aid, send scouts to find them immediately. Experienced attention is needed to save the lives of those who are injured, since ambulances have not yet arrived. Assure to the best of your ability that the first aid being provided in the interim is appropriate.

Help obtain building access. The media truck has stopped in the front entrance of your building. Assign someone to clear the driveway and to direct emergency medical vehicles to the incident area.

Obviously, this is not the end of the list. These are examples to remind you of your several competing critical priorities: for example, the ongoing danger to employees, providing assistance to police, getting effective first aid to victims and facilitating access to emergency medical squads.

Orchestrating Your Response

As a crisis manager, there are too many competing critical needs for you to handle alone. Your job is not to play every instrument in the orchestra. Rather, you are the conductor. Quickly assess priority issues and enlist available persons to take action. Notice in the above list of immediate actions that you delegated every task. Doing so puts you in a position to continue managing the crisis.

This doesn't mean that you never get your hands dirty, but it is hard to manage the whirlwind of a crisis while you are giving CPR to a victim. Only if you are the solitary one qualified for CPR would it be best for you consider direct treatment. Even then, you may want to instruct others in exactly what to do, monitor their techniques for effectiveness and move on.

Now let's take a look at five internal traits that you want to incorporate into your crisis management skills.

- **A state of "deliberate calm."** Requires clear thinking, emotional control and balance.
- **Open-mindedness** as you take in vast amounts of information without developing tunnel vision. Requires keen listening skills.

- **Decisiveness,** balanced with a willingness to consider ideas and input from others. Requires a willingness to prioritize and make decisions with only partial knowledge.
- **Flexibility** to adapt to rapid change and modify your actions. Requires understanding that some (or most) of the early information about critical incidents is wrong.
- **Persuasiveness.** Requires being able to convince others to follow your directions.

The mind is a powerful tool. We have the ability to control our feelings even when the circumstances seem impossible or overwhelming. You can make it through the trials of crisis response if you prepare yourself mentally for the demands that will be placed upon you.

The Imperative for Rapid Response

The period immediately following serious traumatic injury is known as the "golden hour." It's been proven that patients have a far greater chance of successful recovery from their injuries if medical care is delivered within one hour.

A well-planned, frequently reviewed crisis response plan can enable you to respond at top speed, and possibly save people's lives—and the viability of your organization, too. The following are among the tools you need:

Delegate. The only way to manage rapidly emerging consequences following disastrous events is to utilize the resources that are available to you. Your job will be to gather information, assess the situation and quickly establish priorities—and delegate. Be ready to give directives to remote individuals making the notification, on-site managers, available employees and outside resources. Your job is to look out the windshield and steer, not to fix the motor with your head under the hood.

Keep track. Keep a notebook with you at all times during crisis response. Make a habit of writing down information as it comes available, with the times noted in the margin. Write down the names of people you talk with, and the content of the discussions. In the margin, put stars (★) by priority decisions and actions with the approximate time they are to be completed, and arrows (➜) by pending items. Note down the ideas and recommendations that come to mind, for later discussions with management. Of course, it will not be possible to note every action or thought you have in the chaos of an immediate response to a real-life experience like our imagined shooting incident. But as soon as you can, make this invaluable record of your activities and responsibilities.

Do this from initial notification, throughout the entire event up until the disengagement period. Documenting information you receive can help you keep track of all the needed things to do and help protect you or your company if you should be legally challenged about actions you took or your timeliness in responding.

For example, imagine that the family of a victim accuses your company of delaying notification that their loved one had been injured or killed. Your notes can identify the specific times you and they were notified, which could be of critical importance in resolving the dispute. Without documentation of the fact pattern, it can be difficult to defend your actions later. Consult with your attorney regarding how and where to maintain this documentation.

Three Key Questions

One way to prioritize action items in the immediate aftermath is to ask yourself these three questions:

- What needs to *stop* that is presently occurring?
- What needs to *start* that is not presently happening?
- In what ways can this situation *escalate* in severity?

In our shooting scenario above, we needed to *stop* employees from roaming outside the building with a gunman on the loose and emergency services dispatched. We needed to *start* effective first aid and professional life support for the victims as soon as possible. And the situation could *escalate* if the gunman continued to shoot.

Four Categories of Concern

There are four basic areas of concern for senior management, whether in a crisis or during normal business. These topics can also help you identify your action priorities in the early aftermath of a disaster. These are people, business disruption, reputation and finances.

- **People.** No organization is better than its people. Human issues come first, especially when people are injured and deeply impacted. What should be done to address the needs of people? How wide a circle of people is impacted? Who are they? Are they in continuing danger? What information do we need to give and receive from these individuals?
- **Business disruption.** The organization's ability to continue normal productivity will undoubtedly be affected following a catastrophe. This may be due to loss of facilities and equipment, or disruption of employees' ability to work normally. Determine the damage that is irreversible and determine what remains functional. Assess what areas of the organization are inoperable or need to be shut down. Also, determine what work is appropriate to continue. In some cases, as in nuclear plants and other power generating facilities, work must go on. Beware, however, of outrage if you are perceived as putting productivity above the needs of traumatized people. As a general rule, you must address the people needs before the back-to-business needs.
- **Reputation.** In the wake of workplace disasters, there is a tendency for faultfinding. Reporters, journalists, plaintiff attorneys, government regulators, employees, family members, financial analysts and community members may line up to assign blame for negligence. This is a time for honesty and integrity, and also a time to assure you get the best message out to involved publics. In our shooting scenario, the media beat the emergency medical vehicles to the facility. An early priority might be to contact your public relations firm or in-house PR counsel.
- **Finances.** Catastrophe is not a typical budget item. In establishing priorities, you may attempt to consider the financial impact of a crisis not readily contained. Possibly, your insurer, or insurance broker could be helpful in strategies to limit their exposures and yours, as well.

Other Priority-Setting Strategies

Multiple time frames. Yet another means to help you establish priorities is to actually anticipate future developments. The idea is to look at what you anticipate will occur immediately, within minutes, within hours, within the day and longer term. Decisions can be made to respond to and prevent anticipated occurrences.

A balanced approach. Take a balanced approach to decision-making, and examine the situation from various vantage points.

In our shooting scenario, our responses went only as far as addressing the critical items immediately before us. A balanced approach would require not only looking at the details before us, but also consciously taking a "*big picture*" overview of the situation. If the shooter happened to be an employee with a history of making threats that we knew about, a big picture issue might be the collective outrage of those media representatives in our driveway and employees who are now hopefully sequestered in the cafeteria.

Calling legal and public relations professionals may be imperative to address the reputational and financial issues anticipated. Beware that these professionals are often at odds in these situations. Preplanning and agreements on external communications need to be agreed upon during the crisis planning stage.

In prioritizing your initial crisis management actions, ask yourself what information or assessment is needed before proper action can be taken. There can be value in waiting for accurate information. I have been involved with two situations in which fatal corporate air crashes were reported, only to find out later that the tail number on the aircraft was not consistent with that of the plane reported down. Had families of those on the manifest been notified, the fallout would have been devastating.

If you have established and trained a crisis management team, they will be available to assist you in prioritizing vital decisions and actions. However, in the early moments following a critical incident, before they can assemble, ask yourself what needs to be decided immediately. What needs input from other disciplines? For example, if a crime is involved you would *not* want to make decisions to begin immediate cleanup of the crime scene. You would need to get input from assets protection, security or law enforcement first.

As a general rule, your job is to act on critical items that can't wait for the team to assemble and discuss. But remember: The best decisions are typically made by small, multidisciplinary teams trained and experienced in crisis management.

Checklist of Immediate Action Items

Your Checklist of Immediate Actions can vary widely according to the incident. A kidnap and ransom situation will involve an immediate call to your insurer or an organization who specializes in hostage negotiations. A toxic chemical plume over a neighboring community would require an immediate call to the mayor or city administrator.

Add to the generic list below according to your culture, anticipated critical incidents, geographic location and other applicable variables.

- **Continuing Danger.** Take action to protect anyone in harm's way.
- **Emergency Vehicles.** Verify dispatch in sufficient quantities; assure access to incident areas.
- **Assessment and Verification.** What information needs to be verified? What immediate information do you need to better assess the situation?
- **Security.** Secure the incident area and perimeter; control ingress and egress; determine how many security personnel are needed; where they are to be placed and for how long; establish who can be put in place until additional security arrives; armed or unarmed; arrest capability or professional guard service?
- **Families.** Do families of victims need to be notified? By whom? How? Convey to employees what to say and not say to families and others calling in. Determine where calls from family members of casualties should be forwarded. Anticipate the needs of family members arriving on site.
- **Escalation.** How can this situation get worse? What can be done to prevent escalation?
- **Notifications.** Who needs to be immediately notified for assistance? Establish a protocol.
- **Communications.** What communications are necessary? To whom? What communications need to be received? From whom?

What methods should be used? What are our main messages for various audiences?

- **Legal and Regulatory.** What immediate legal or regulatory compliance issues need to be addressed?
- **Specialists.** What internal and external specialists should be contacted immediately for assistance? Technical experts? Crisis mental health professionals? Toxic exposure? Environmental? Medical? Communications? Safety?

In establishing your own checklist, determine if you want to make a generic list that covers "all" foreseeable risks or create separate lists for each type of catastrophic incident. In some cases, it's better to have a combination of generic and specific lists.

Even with years of experience in crisis management consulting, I still refer to my lists. I want pilots on flights I take to refer to their "lists" no matter how many times they have flown the jet! If I were CEO of your organization, I would want my crisis managers to do the same.

There's no question that taking the right immediate action steps is a heady responsibility. But by breaking it down as we have in this chapter, you should be in a much better position to know what you face.

In Chapter Four, we'll move on to the process of informing those on your notification lists. Additionally, we'll look at what many crisis-prepared companies are doing to address humanitarian response needs in the wake of catastrophes.

Quick Use Response Guide

CHAPTER 3: IMMEDIATE ACTIONS, INITIAL RESPONSE PHASE

❑ Continuing Danger?
   ✓ Take action to protect anyone in danger.

❑ Emergency Vehicles
   ✓ Verify dispatch and sufficient quantities.
   ✓ Dispatch those trained in first aid in the interim.
   ✓ Provide direction and assistance for arriving emergency vehicles.

❑ Assessment and Verification
   ✓ What information needs to be verified to take appropriate action?
   ✓ What communications do you need to receive?

❑ Security
   ✓ Do you need security to protect the incident area?
   ✓ Secure the perimeter of the work site?
   ✓ What areas of ingress and egress need to be secured?
   ✓ How much security is needed? Where? How long?
   ✓ Armed or unarmed?
   ✓ Arrest capability or professional guard service?
   ✓ Who can you put in place until security arrives?

❑ Evaluate the need to temporarily close part or the entire site.

❑ Families
   ✓ Do families of victims need to be notified? By whom? How?
   ✓ Response to telephone inquires? By whom?
   ✓ To whom should inquiries from family members be directed?
   ✓ Assign personnel to immediately meet and direct family members who may arrive onsite?

❑ Escalation
   ✓ How can this situation escalate in severity?
   ✓ What is being done to respond to or prevent escalation?

❑ Notification
   ✓ Who needs to be immediately notified for assistance?
   ✓ Establish a protocol.

❑ Communication
   ✓ What communications are necessary? To whom?
   ✓ What communications need to be received? By whom?
   ✓ What method of assistance is needed?
   ✓ What are the main messages you want to convey to various audiences?

❑ Legal and Regulatory
    ✓ Immediate compliance issues to address?

❑ Specialists
    ✓ What internal and external specialists should you contact?
    ✓ Technical experts?
    ✓ Crisis mental health professionals?
    ✓ Toxic exposure?
    ✓ Environmental?
    ✓ Medical?
    ✓ Safety?
    ✓ Communications?
    ✓ Others?

CHAPTER 4

Informing Others and Humanitarian Response

Now you face the all-important task of informing others of the situation. You need to turn a page with scribbled names and numbers into an action-oriented checklist that will guide you through the process of notifying individuals and mobilizing those who will help your company through this crisis.

It isn't enough to spread the word. You have to share essential information, and elicit additional knowledge from those who matter most. In this chapter you'll learn about:

- Creating an Integrated Notification Plan
- Giving and getting critical information
- Making death or serious injury notifications to next-of-kin
- Establishing a Humanitarian Response Team

Notification vs. Mobilization

You must determine whether you are calling people to simply *notify* them, or to *mobilize* them into action. It's a critically important distinction. Only if you're sure why you're calling can you expect those you reach to know what's expected of them.

Assume that you work for a global energy company at the home office. Over a thousand miles from the headquarters, one of your oil rig employees in Ecuador has gone missing. Coworkers reported that he did not show up for third shift with the others in his group and he can't be found in the compound.

Understanding the foreseeable risk of kidnapping that stems from the political environment in which these workers operate, you determined that your CEO should be notified. The call is made to his home, just after midnight. He is clearly concerned, but pleased to have been informed. He asks you to monitor the situation personally and confidentially over the next two hours before any further steps are taken.

No one is mobilized in this case due to the fact pattern. If the employee was known for going into the nearby town of Lago Agrio for extended periods and having a few beers, or if he had been missing before, the mobilization of the Crisis Management Team and others may be delayed. If this is out of character for him, or there is evidence of foul play, then mobilization of company would be indicated.

Other scenarios may be less clear-cut and require you to make more subtle distinctions between notification and mobilization. The checklists I provide in this book will help you cut through the confusion of the moment; use them as tools to keep yourself focused and effective. You will find a fairly comprehensive list of possible notification contacts below.

Beyond Phone Numbers

An essential component of a notification plan is the list of phone numbers. Agree on exactly how everyone on the "needs to know" list will be alerted. Have backup people, with numbers, for each individual on the list. An administrative person or outside vendor should keep your list of key phone numbers always pristinely up to date.

Your internal voice mail system could be used as a resource for rapid notifications. Many systems can be programmed to leave broadcast messages for predefined groups, though a disadvantage is that you won't know if someone didn't receive the notification.

For key individuals, such as members of senior management, the list should indicate how the person prefers to be notified, for example: first by cell phone; in the middle of the night, only in certain circumstances; only when certain thresholds have been met.

For example, if there is a hurricane with multiple businesses and residences demolished, the immediate needs of your public relations person are not as paramount as when yours is the only company affected by a disaster. Ideally, you would have a notification list that included the core people to be informed, plus the specialty list according to the needs of each foreseeable incident.

It is likely that you will need to immediately notify your Crisis Management Team (CMT) members, senior management, various key staff positions and possibly even the board of directors. Let's look at essential notification information for several of these.

Key Contacts

The list of potential key notification contacts includes the following:

- Crisis Management Team members
- Senior management
- Board of directors
- Administrative staff, including:
  - Legal
  - Security/assets protection
  - PR/communications
  - Human resources
  - Employee relations
  - Risk and insurance management
  - Facilities
  - Finance
  - Benefits
  - Medical
- Employees and their families
- Law enforcement
- Customers
- Distributors
- Franchisees
- Financial and stock analysts
- Government regulators
- Industry activist groups
- Industry associations
- Business partners
- Media representatives and spokespersons

- Union representatives
- Suppliers
- Consultants (crisis management professionals, legal, security, EAP [Employee Assistance Program], mental health specialists, technical specialists, medical spokespeople, PR, industry specialists)
- Insurance companies
- Third-party administrator
- Insurance broker
- Hospitals
- Community contacts
- Local and national elected officials
- U.S. or other embassies
- Retained technical experts
- Retained medical or public health professionals
- Repair services
- Cleanup crews
- Your own family

Let's go into some detail on a few of the primary contacts:

Crisis management team. An immediate decision to make is whether to put your team on notice, or fully mobilize them. If the decision is to mobilize, this should be a relatively straightforward process. If CMT members are at their homes during off hours, contact those who live the furthest away before members who live nearby, to give them extra time to reach the assembly point. You and they should be in agreement about their roles, their ability to work together and their aptitude for taking action when confronted by critical incidents.

Depending on the size of your organization, you will have a core CMT of five to ten people. But for every foreseeable risk, there will likely be auxiliary team members you call in as needed.

Auxiliary team members might include a health care specialist, law enforcement officer, attorney, crisis management professional, public relations, industrial hygienist, hazardous materials (hazmat) expert, etc.

As you develop your notification plan, ask questions like: "If we have a chemical plume hanging overhead, what special expertise might we need?" The answer might be, for example, a specialty physician to make determinations about health risks to workers and members of the community. An expert on the chemical itself (say, from the Centers for Disease Control) might be most appropriate, or perhaps key individuals from the municipality with whom you will coordinate any evacuations, joint communications, or the like.

During the notification/mobilization process, your duty vis-à-vis these auxiliary experts is to apprise them of the situation, clearly delineate the information or action steps you expect of them and come to an understanding about when and how these requirements will be carried out.

Taking It to the Top

As you make notifications, you may run into a fairly common scenario. That is a tendency for the individual charged with notifying senior management (possibly you, as the crisis manager) to delay notification of top brass in order to learn more about what's really happened and to investigate why the incident occurred. It's only natural that your CEO will have immediate questions and you will want to be prepared to answer them. But sometimes you just can't. It is many times more important to notify early and answer, "I don't know," than to wait to cover all the bases before notification.

Waiting too long to notify top leaders about a crisis can dangerously delay the application of essential corporate resources to the problem.

Board of directors. Although board members do not typically play an active role in the day-to-day operations of most companies, they do have major responsibility for the organization and its well-being. Notifying board members can help you manage the crisis and minimize detriment, depending on your board's areas of influence and expertise.

Most often, the CEO is the one who notifies the board. In any case, senior management should determine the threshold for contacting board members in the immediate aftermath of the crisis. The threshold for contacting the board of directors can be defined ahead of time, or when management feels that their input would be beneficial. If there is a significant financial, reputational or business resumption threat to the company, the board probably will want to be notified sooner rather than later.

What information might you need from board members? It depends, again, on the imminent risk and the type of crisis. Are there high level contacts in the industry or in government who could help the company manage a response to a catastrophic incident? Board members are chosen for their many contacts, industry-related expertise, or other valuable experience they have. Their input and assistance can be invaluable.

Staff positions. In nearly every imaginable scenario, your corporate counsel would figure high on the call list. Crises are high probability times for litigation. Containment of liability exposures will be essential as you move through the post-crisis period.

Depending on your culture, the lawyer may become the designated spokesperson. However, this can give the impression that the company is only interested in minimizing legal exposures. Whether your attorney is your spokesperson or not, there is an inherent conflict between legal and public relations concerns. Attorneys are concerned about minimizing communications that could increase liability. Public relations personnel are communicators who want to get clear and timely messages out to reduce misunderstandings and to tell the company's side of the story.

Another reason for early notification of your attorney is safeguarding evidence. Should a member of the legal staff be on hand to assure that there were no improprieties or any kind of tampering? Coordinating early defense decisions with your insurer and appointed defense attorneys is yet another action that your legal staff needs to address. Now is the time to find out what your attorney would want according to each foreseeable risk.

If your company's headquarters is at a considerable distance from the site of the crisis, it may be of immediate importance to retain a local law firm to represent your interests there.

The list of staff to notify goes on from there. Your security/assets protection manager will no doubt have a significant part to play in the immediate post-crisis response. Determine in advance what this person will need to know. Anticipate questions such as, *"Is a crime suspected?"* and *"Is the perimeter of the facility secure?"* In turn, what do you need to know from him or her? Your immediate security actions can make a huge difference in your defensibility. If you allow evidence to be contaminated, there may be a lingering perception that you are culpable. Timely notification and coordination with your security department will help your organization take critical defensive action.

As you can see, the list includes customers, vendors, franchisees, trade groups, unions, financial analysts, silent partners, insurers, government agencies, remediation services and even your own family. Don't underestimate the impact crisis response may have on you, the crisis manager! It is more exhausting and demanding than you may have imagined.

Giving Essential Information

Whomever you're addressing—whether it's the CEO, your benefits manager, HR vice president or a representative of the media, think back to the four essential information-seeking questions we introduced in Chapter Two. These cover the basic facts and are what most people, those assisting you and those reporting on you, will want to know:

- What happened?
- How bad is it?
- What is being done?
- What is the potential for escalation?

You asked these questions when you received the initial notification. Now you need to convey what you learned as you are informing those on your immediate call list.

Let's turn our attention to additional notifications that must be made in the early aftermath of a workplace incident where people are killed or seriously injured.

Notifying Next-of-Kin

You might assume that law enforcement or a coroner's office would take care of notifying relatives of persons fatally injured in a workplace tragedy. This is especially true in the United Kingdom. But even there, law enforcement has readily welcomed the willingness of corporate managers to accompany them during death notifications. Whatever the culture, it's a mistake to assume that you can simply pass the duty of death notification on to law enforcement or medical personnel.

Although fundamentally unpleasant, it is imperative that such notification be done correctly. You only have one opportunity to do it right; any mistakes will be remembered for a lifetime by you—and by the affected family members.

Unfortunately, I have heard many horror stories about next-of-kin notifications "gone bad." One manager was faced with the task of notifying the spouses of three workers involved in a gas company explosion—one had died and the other two were hospitalized with burns. The facility was located in a small town and, as is common in such communities, the manager knew all three spouses. He chose to notify the wife of the fatality first at her at home. Upon hearing the news, she was understandably overcome. She pleaded with the manager to stay with her and threw her arms around his neck, wailing in shock and grief. To her great outrage, the manager promptly tore himself away—his sense of duty compelled him to reach the other two spouses, knowing they would want to rush to the hospital to see their loves ones, perhaps for the last time.

In order to avoid such a costly emotional blunder, the manager should have quickly selected other employees or managers to accompany him to the house as he shared the horrific news. Or, better yet, managers could have been chosen to independently notify the three families. This would not have been hard to do in a small community, and it would have assured that the devastated widow not be left alone.

Guidance to help notifiers avoid some of these mistakes is provided below.

Next-of-Kin Notification Guidelines

- Remind all managers and employees not to release the names of the deceased to the media until immediate survivors are notified.
- If an individual is critically injured and death is imminent, make the notification as soon as possible, even by phone, to allow the family members an opportunity to spend final moments with their loved one.
- Make death notifications in person, preferably accompanied by someone else. Another person can help share the emotional burden and help manage emotional reactions, including possible hostility. Two notifiers can also substantiate the details of the visit, if necessary.

- Ask to enter the home. *Never* make a death notification on the doorstep!
- Ask those present to sit down. Do not sit in Dad's recliner, especially if he is the one killed. Pull up a dining room chair if possible.
- Be factual, honest, direct and caring. Get to the point quickly. *Do not* communicate a false sense of hope. Use words like "dead," or "died" rather than "lost" or "passed on."
- Be supportive if family members react with hysteria, weeping, anger, shock, etc. If you believe hostility or physical violence might ensue, arrange to be accompanied by a law enforcement officer. As a rule, it is best to sit nearest the door, if possible.
- If family members wish to go to the hospital, encourage them not to drive themselves. Drive them or arrange for transportation.
- Be prepared to make appropriate arrangements if there are young children in the home. One of the notifiers could stay with the children until other family, friends or neighbors arrive to care for them.
- If the next-of-kin are away from home or out of town, you are still responsible for notifying them. However you reach them, the same rules apply.
- Arrange for a high-ranking company official to personally contact the family as soon as crisis management demands allow. This can be quite reassuring and serves to demonstrate the company's sensitivity and caring.
- If your company has a program which designates people to assist family members with their needs and communications to and from the company following an incident—typically called family representatives—it's best to have other individuals do a death notification. You don't want the family representatives who are assigned the role of assisting family members to be thought of as the messenger who brought the bad news.

A Team with Heart

One means to assist you or others responsible for next-of-kin notification is to establish a team separate from the CMT that is charged with managing this and other humanitarian aspects of a crisis.

Even the best Crisis Management Teams can easily become over-whelmed by the business needs and physical content of a crisis. The ten-dency, thus, is to overlook people who may have averted physical injury. As we all learned following the terrorist attacks on America, one does not have to be injured physically to be traumatized.

A Humanitarian Response Team should be considered as an adjunct to your Crisis Management Team. This is a group specially trained and inter-ested in assisting with the emotional, communication, logistical and adjust-ment needs of those affected by the crisis. Those who witnessed the event, people injured, surviving family members, non-injured employees, by-standers, community members and anyone else associated with the com-pany who feels overwhelmed or needs support in the wake of the events would be under the caring assistance of this Humanitarian Response Team. Tasks they could orchestrate include:

○ Next-of-kin notifications
○ Identification of at-risk individuals
○ Emotional first aid
○ De-escalation meeting with employees prior to going home
○ Initial psychological support for those severely impacted
○ Family representatives dispatched to impacted families
○ Communications between impacted families and the company
○ Requests and needs for families of casualties
○ Psychological support (group debriefings, individual assessment and counseling, EAP, etc.)
○ Funerals and memorials
○ Emergency travel assistance
○ Benefits issues
○ Financial assistance for impacted workers and their families
○ Continued family assistance
○ International medi-vac transport services
○ Work normalization assistance (including authorizing absence with pay)
○ Back-to-work transitions
○ Outreach, volunteer and giving programs

It is easy to overlook the myriad people-related needs during a crisis re-sponse. That is why an increasing number of companies are creating Humanitarian Response Teams. Your organization may be well served to follow suit. Four months after the 2001 terrorism upon America, the Reputation Institute observed:

> The more impressed people were with the corporate response to September 11th in general, the more positively they rated companies' reputations across each of the six areas of reputation—emotional appeal, financial performance, products and services, vision and leadership, social responsibility, and workplace environment. Not only was the public impressed by the corporate response, but also most felt that companies' actions made them more "human" and more "sensitive."

In Chapter Five, we'll discuss ways to assemble the team that's going to help you respond to the crisis with ability, compassion and timeliness. We'll also visit the place they will meet, the Crisis Command Center.

Quick Use Response Guide

CHAPTER 4: INFORMING OTHERS AND HUMANITARIAN RESPONSE

- Have you implemented a Notification Plan that:
  - ○ Considers who should be notified?
  - ○ Identifies what information should be communicated *to* each source?
  - ○ Identifies what information is needed *from* each source?
- Have you determined the thresholds that indicate notification vs. mobilization, especially regarding members of your Crisis Management Team?
- Have you reviewed the Key Contacts List to determine which are most relevant to your given crisis, and established protocol for enlisting each?
- Have you established next-of-kin notification procedures that include:
  - ○ Who will make such notification?
  - ○ Key steps as outlined in the notification guidelines?

○ Training and guidance for those who would serve in this notification capacity?
- Has a group of employee volunteers been selected, trained and dispatched as family representatives to serve the needs of families of casualties?
- Have you established a Humanitarian Response Team that is an adjunct to your Crisis Management Team to assist with the emotional and communications needs of affected people?

CHAPTER 5

Mobilizing Your Team:
Crisis Containment Phase

We're now entering the "crisis containment phase."

The right place and the right people—plus the right planning—will enable your orderly, effective response. From Ground Zero in New York City to the Oklahoma City bomb site, to Hurricane Andrew, to kidnapped oil workers in the Ecuadorian jungle, a deliberate approach to crisis containment can make all the difference.

In this chapter, we'll focus on three main points:

- The Crisis Command Center
- The role of the Crisis Management Team (CMT) leader
- The initial CMT meeting and action steps

Scouting Your Location

Sometimes they are called Emergency Operations Centers (EOCs) or Emergency Response Rooms (ERRs), but we will refer to the nerve center of your crisis response as the Crisis Command Center.

Identifying the location for your Crisis Command Center is an essential first step. You may find that the space you ultimately choose was not your first choice, or is less than ideal. But I've seen highly effective responses even from small, cramped quarters. And I've witnessed astoundingly marginal responses from spacious, well-equipped spaces. The goal is to identify and retain an excellent location that's sizable, accommodates the needed technology and is strategically located.

High-risk operations, like chemical companies, nuclear facilities and oil and gas companies, tend to have sophisticated Crisis Command Centers. Simply put, they're more likely to need them than a real estate company or a financial services operation. What do these facilities look like? Just envision a smaller version of the television images you've seen of NASA's control center: a sleek, high-tech operation including computer workstations and phone banks staffed by alert teams.

More common are less elaborate centers, such as a room with tables arranged in a horseshoe configuration that permits everyone to share the same view of the front; or, a typical conference room with a large table. The room is equipped with white boards, or perhaps mounted easel pads strategically placed for all to see.

The ideal room is well equipped technologically, with capability for sending and receiving faxes (possibly separate lines for each); multiple phone lines; computers with e-mail and Web access; television monitors with cable or satellite capabilities and VCRs; two-way radios; and video conferencing. Don't forget to include one decidedly low-tech communication device—a bullhorn!

On the non-technological side, adjacent rooms might have some cots for catnaps by team members or other key players who are on extended service. It is good to be near restrooms, a kitchen or other food service. And it should have controlled access. An open, bullpen-style space, for example, is a huge challenge because of the inherent difficulty of controlling traffic in and out.

Many companies opt for a space that offers one or more break-out rooms—smaller nearby rooms in which senior management or other individuals can gather and work comfortably. Media and communications personnel typically have a separate adjacent room to monitor news and create written communications.

Other Possibilities

Perhaps this level of accommodation is not available to you. Your business may not even have a computer-connected training room or other convertible space. Alternatives include a board or conference room, or even a plant manager's office. These can be adequate.

Several years ago, Coca-Cola Enterprises faced a catastrophic incident in McAllen, Texas. Tragically, a school bus carrying eighty-one students collided with a Coca-Cola delivery truck. The bus veered into an excavation pit partially filled with water, and twenty-one students drowned in the accident. Although the event captured national media attention, the company was able to successfully manage this event from a small Crisis Command Center in the local manager's office, maintaining excellent communications with the community. Within days, Coca-Cola Enterprises was recognized in the community for their effective crisis response, and sales of Coca-Cola in the area actually increased following the tragic incident. Clearly, excellent crisis management is possible even from makeshift facilities.

Whatever space you designate, you should call for a "gatekeeper" who is not part of the Crisis Management Team, whose sole purpose is to manage traffic in and out of the room. This person should be armed with a list of team members, backups and invited experts. If sensitive information is posted on the walls, it makes sense that only authorized personnel should be allowed into the room. There's no question that things can get a little crazy in your command center. The importance of controlling traffic cannot be overstated.

It is vital during an actual emergency for Crisis Management Team members to receive important information from arriving personnel and to delegate actions to selected outsiders who need direction. The gatekeeper should balance that need for people and information coming into and going out of the Crisis Command Center with the potential for distractions and the opportunity for chaos.

You'll also want to appoint several runners to deliver messages or items between the Crisis Command Center and other places, like other offices in the building, a press center, municipal offices, the police or fire department, etc. They also tackle tasks assigned by the CMT. This is an important function that keeps the Crisis Management Team cohesive and at the table. Without runners, there is a tendency for the team to disperse as members race to cover needed tasks.

Sharing Pertinent Information

One of the primary purposes of your Crisis Command Center is to serve as a large-scale kiosk, a place to receive, post and respond to information about the events as they transpire. At a minimum, three primary types of information should be displayed visually. These are:

- The evolving fact pattern
- Priority actions
- Pending items

Information is the raw material of which your crisis response is crafted. The quality, accuracy and timeliness of that information will greatly affect your response. Let's examine these types of information individually.

The Evolving Fact Pattern

At first blush, "evolving fact pattern" might appear a contradiction in terms. But when the subject is a flash flood, a bombing, a plane crash or an industrial accident, a fact pattern can turn on a dime. "Solid" tips become misinformation, and facts that appeared fully corroborated can vaporize as new input is gathered.

Posting of the evolving fact pattern is essential. It should occupy a highly visible spot in the room. Some companies have developed preprinted easel sheets or prepared white boards to organize needed information and tracking. Use a grid (see illustration below) that spells out the following:

- The facts
- Date and time of entry
- Verified or not (a check-off box)
- By whom

Date: _____

Emerging Facts	Time Entered	Verified	By Whom

Although these key facts must be written in big, bold handwriting (or type) so that they can be seen from twenty or more feet away, ancillary information can be entered into the grid in smaller print. Periodically, the information should be turned over to another designee, a "scribe," who will assure that every entry is ultimately uploaded into a central collection point. This can be as simple as turning easel pages over to someone sitting at a laptop who captures the information for safekeeping. This practice should be completed not only for the evolving fact pattern, but for priority actions and pending items that are also posted in the Crisis Command Center.

It's important that the task of noting incoming information be assigned to a reliable individual outside the Crisis Management Team. Look for someone with excellent organizational skills, highly readable handwriting, good stamina and the ability to remain cool under pressure. An ideal choice is an unflappable administrative staffer who works quickly, is not bothered by multiple voices barking out constantly changing instructions and will not fall apart under pressure.

Priority Actions

The second type of information that must be maintained is priority actions. These are the steps that must be taken by your Crisis Management Team members, and others within and beyond the organization, to move forward.

This grid is relatively simple—you want to chart the action, the responsible person, and the time by which the action will be taken. Simply mark through those items that have been completed. An option would be to have a check-off box for each item to indicate completed tasks.

Date: _____

Priority Actions	Responsible Person	Deadline

Like the fact pattern, the priority actions evolve and change. After you've gotten your employees and guests out of a burning building, other priorities move to the top of the list, such as notifying next-of-kin of casualties, and setting up a press statement. Unfortunately, one priority doesn't always wait for the next. In reality, all three of these actions—evacuation, family notifications and press statement—probably need to be executed very soon, provided you ensure that any press statement with names happens only after next of kin are notified.

Pending Items

During a crisis (or a simulation), you can expect a steady flow of entries to pass from the pending items list to the priority actions list. For example, your chief executive officer must make a visit to a distraught family who has lost a loved one in a workplace shooting. But it goes on the pending items list—the priority is sending a trained member of your Family Representative Team there immediately. The CEO visit will become a priority later.

The immediate aftermath of a crisis is not the time for your CEO to show up on the doorstep. Especially not while the media and the board of directors are demanding attention and information. The family is in deep shock and, following proper notification as described in Chapter Four, needs to retreat as the news sinks in.

As facts and circumstances change, pending items will become priorities and, eventually, make their way off the list.

Additional Command Center Tips

As mentioned above, the evolving fact pattern, priority actions and pending items must be captured in a permanent manner by your scribe. This type of paper trail is important for purposes of legal documentation. This documentation serves as an invaluable reference when questions arise during crisis response. What you wrote down and what was accomplished when and by whom is also of great importance as you conduct your debriefing after the crisis. Some of the most important lessons will come from this documentation. It will be up to your legal counsel to determine the format and how much crisis response documentation your organization will produce and maintain. It is advisable to compile all notes into a single and final set of documentation that is approved and housed by your attorney. All extraneous notes should be destroyed as a matter of policy and standard procedure.

Consider these additional considerations for a high-functioning Crisis Command Center:

- It is best to have everyone maintain phone logs of calls that come into the Crisis Command Center. These logs can be an invaluable reference when captured in a consistent format. And it's really the only definitive way to determine if a particular call was actually made or received. The log should be compiled as long as your Crisis Command Center is operational. It is best to capture:
  - who called and when
  - to whom
  - the nature of the call
  - the phone number
- Your Humanitarian Response Team should have an established site of operation. This can be in a separate room, adjacent or quite close to the Crisis Command Center; or, space permitting, within the command center. These people need mental and physical space for the

very tough job of managing the people issues. If the Crisis Command Center is too small and does not provide adequate space free from distractions, choose another room in the building. Use available means—cell phones, runners, instant messaging, etc.—to exchange messages and update information between the two locations. The purpose of this separation is to keep the Humanitarian Response Team members away from the physical content side of the crisis. Their job is exclusively the people side.

• Keep your Crisis Management Team members focused. I've observed a tendency for team members to jump up to accomplish tasks, such as running down needed information, or seek personnel files. If Harry's errand keeps him away from the Crisis Command Center for fifteen minutes, you've lost a quarter hour of input. Then, Sue is off on a thirty-minute task, and Steve, your team leader, is making phone calls back in his office. Before you know it, your team has disappeared and its ability to manage the crisis has been compromised. Keep team members in place and assure that there are sufficient runners.

During a simulation at a private middle school, the headmaster, a member of the Crisis Management Team, decided to meet the family of an injured child. He then left the command center. A couple of minutes later he returned, but I put him in the corner—something I had always wanted to do as a student. He was not allowed to give input because he was now "gone" to the hospital. Why? In a "real life" crisis, he could never have made his way to the hospital, met with the family and returned in two minutes. His absence was keenly felt and valuable input was lost while he was out. Someone else could easily have accomplished that contact with the family, as important as it was. There was time later when the crisis was successfully contained for the headmaster to visit the hospital.

Hopefully, you now have a good idea what a Crisis Command Center looks like, what its purpose is and how it should operate. Building on the mistake of the middle school headmaster, we turn our attention next to the role of the Crisis Management Team leader.

Taking Charge

Your leader needs to be empowered—by policy and by practice—to take action. Of course, the ability to collaborate and delegate are also essential, but your leader needs authority that is broad enough to permit him or her to function effectively.

Making order out of chaos is a fairly unusual "job description," but it precisely describes the job of the leader. This is someone who can manage noise, uncertainty, stress, fear and grief, in the midst of disaster—while simultaneously conveying calm and stability.

Those who are old enough—or who watch re-runs—are familiar with the plate-spinner, a frequent guest on TV variety shows like Ed Sullivan of the 1950s and 60s. This individual gets multiple plates spinning on wooden dowels and, magically, manages to run among them, giving each just enough tweak to keep it in the air, while looking out for the next wobbling plate and rushing to its rescue. Miraculously, none comes crashing down. This type of person—armed with planning, training and a supportive and capable team—is your ideal leader.

Follow the Leader

A common scenario to be avoided involves the tension between the team leader and the CEO. Here's what I mean. Typically, when companies are in a crisis, there is someone like a risk manager or corporate counsel leading the response. But then the CEO instinctively decides to do what he or she always does—lead. Suddenly, this individual is there with sleeves rolled up, making unilateral decisions. Ideally, your CEO will choose to be involved, but under the direction of the Crisis Management Team leader. The enlightened senior executives will go to the team leader and ask how they can help. Make no mistake—the senior officers are the leaders of your company at all times in all situations. But effective leadership is achieved through orderly and clear designation of roles and responsibilities—and that includes permitting the Crisis Management Team leader to lead and the CMT to work as a unit.

The Initial Crisis Management Team Meeting

The immediate goal of the initial Crisis Management Team meeting is to communicate the needed facts to team members and their alternates. Alternates might also gather in the Crisis Command Center, but perhaps not at the team table.

Remember the basic questions that should seem familiar by now—what happened, how bad is it, what is being done and what is the escalation potential?

The team leader should facilitate the discussion, keep it moving and on track. Take the opportunity during this session to briefly discuss the issues and to assign priority items. *Crisis management is active.* It is what the team actively does—like communicating and dispatching resources—that contains a crisis.

This is also the time to set the tone for the management of the crisis. This is best done by assuring that key decisions have been made and will be respected. Among these:

- Means of communication to and from the team leader. No Crisis Management Team can function any better than the communications it gives and receives.
- A series of checks and balances. Keep track of activities, who will take responsibility for each, and by when.
- Established priorities for the team leader's involvement that delineates which decisions must be made with his or her involvement, and which can be made by others.
- Tasks that will be delegated to others outside the team.
- Decisions that will require senior management approval.

Valuable Lessons

Here are some recommendations I made for members of one Crisis Management Team, after its first crisis response simulation. Your team can benefit from them, too.

1. Refer to your manual from the outset to assure that key points are covered in a timely way.
2. Encourage members to use the focused imagery technique, especially when planning interactions with deeply affected family members.
3. Prioritize actions, not just information, to speed up handling of initial crisis management needs. This applies to humanitarian as well as other crisis content actions.
4. The initial meeting (and subsequent ones) took too long; make priorities and dispense with extraneous details.
5. Avoid too much monologue by the team leader—not enough team decision-making.
6. Focus your communications on action items; if no action is needed, move on to the next item.
7. Use periodic time-outs! This is a means of taking control of the process (and managing the chaos) and making sure the left hand knows what the right hand is doing.
8. Team members should stay in control of phone calls by keeping them short, get others to take and receive calls and insist that callers get to the point, then let you go.
9. Delegate as much as appropriate so that the team can continue to "look out the windshield" at where you are headed. Avoid getting bogged down in the details that others can handle.

Interestingly, this Crisis Management Team adequately handled every one of these issues in their second simulation. Practice pays off.

In Chapter Six, we'll dig deeper into the team and its duties.

Quick Use Response Guide

CHAPTER 5: MOBILIZING YOUR TEAM: CRISIS CONTAINMENT PHASE

- Crisis Command Center
  - Have you identified and prepared a room for the Crisis Management Team to meet during crisis response?
    - Extended hours capabilities

- Alternative off-site location, if needed
- Posted security guard/gatekeeper

○ Is the room configured for maximum efficiency?
- Information posted visibly
- Proper ventilation

○ Is it technologically connected?
- Presently equipped
- Ready to be retrofitted

○ Possible equipment in the Crisis Command Center
- Fax machine to receive
- Fax machine to send (separate line)
- Multiple phone lines (with some unpublished numbers separate from the normal phone system)
  - Phone headsets
  - Speaker phone
- Chargers for cell phones
- Computers with e-mail and Internet capabilities
  - PC network
- LAN printer
- Television monitors and VCRs
- Satellite or cable television connections
- Two-way radios
- Video conferencing capabilities
- Box of office supplies
- Defibrillator (just in case the stress leads to heart attack)
- Flashlight and other emergency equipment
- Bullhorn

○ Has a method been established for visually posting pertinent information on easels, white boards, PowerPoint, etc.?
- Emerging facts
- Priority actions
- Pending items
- Digital photographs
- Other pertinent information

• Crisis Management Team Leader
○ Is the team leader empowered with the authority and access to senior management that is necessary to fulfill the duties of crisis response?

- Have a sufficient number of runners and assistants been designated for delegation so the leader can keep the Crisis Management Team together?
- Initial Crisis Management Team meeting
  - Have a method established for documentation.
  - Establish a phone log system.
  - Generate a sufficient number of methods for communications to and from the team.
  - Utilize checklists for immediate team considerations (according to the incident at hand).
- Humanitarian Response Team
  - Utilize this team to exclusively address the myriad people-related issues of a traumatic or distressing incident.
  - Locate the Humanitarian Response Team near the Crisis Management Team to facilitate coordination between the two teams.
  - The CMT leader will delegate any people-related issues to the Humanitarian Response Team for implementation and follow-up.
  - Assign one person on the CMT to serve as the liaison between the Humanitarian Response Team and the CMT.

CHAPTER 6

Creating Order Out of Chaos

At this point, the Crisis Management Team has positioned itself onto the front lines and is prepared to do battle. The team is ensconced in its bunker (the Crisis Command Center). It has established methods of communication (white boards, runners, phones, faxes, e-mail, etc.) internally and with the outside. Everyone knows who's in command. There are plenty of sandwiches, coffee and supplies available.

And that's good, because you could be in for a long siege.

In this chapter, the focus turns to the "orderly" process of relieving chaos. I use the word orderly with caution because when push comes to shove, crisis management can become pretty frenzied. We will cover:

- Identifying the real crisis
- Administering emotional first aid
- Holding the de-escalation meeting

Understanding the Crisis

To start, you must identify the crisis. At first blush, that would appear obvious. It's the shooting, flood, the fire or the explosion, right? Not necessarily. Returning briefly to the September 11th terrorist attacks could lead us to a different conclusion.

The crisis that would grip the overall crisis managers (Mayor Rudolph Giuliani and his lieutenants) for months to come was not the damage to the two towers. No amount of preparedness, timely action or management savvy could change the fact that the buildings had been hit. The part of the crisis that they could address lay before them in horrific, graphic detail. It was the need for evacuation, tending to injuries, and dislocation: people who were hurt or in harm's way, had lost loved ones, just watched, or took part in the rescue. The human ripple effect was enormous. Giuliani's team recognized this distinction quickly and wisely. One sign of that recognition was the fact that the mayor enlisted a cameraman and a willing network and began immediately to communicate with the public.

Whether your crisis involves multiple deaths and injuries, or "only" involves a life-threatening experience, the steps you take to manage the humanitarian side are the same. In either case, people will be deeply affected and looking for a caring, compassionate response. Depending on your crisis management structure, this process is shepherded either by the Crisis Management Team itself, or by a Humanitarian Response Team. It's also possible that the crisis is being managed from afar—perhaps from headquarters where the corporate CMT is directing the action.

The term "emotional first aid" refers to the *initial management response* associated with addressing the people side of crisis. Emotional first aid can include a number of actions.

- Accounting for everyone and conveying information to loved ones and associates
- Enlisting the help to assist you and your team in controlling disorder and confusion
- Protecting employees and others from exposure to additional traumatic sights and experiences
- Making contact with victims, witnesses and others experiencing traumatic stress reactions
- Helping to meet immediate needs, from contacting loved ones to offering a blanket and physical comforting
- Giving those affected good information about what has happened
- Providing a "buddy system" for support in coping during the early aftermath

Rallying the Troops

An intuitive first step is to rally your troops. It is best to set up a location for everyone to gather so that you can determine who's accounted for and who's not. When assigning an emergency meeting place, make sure to have a backup location in case the primary spot has become inaccessible.

Unfortunately, accounting for everyone may be a difficult task. After Hurricane Andrew, one building where approximately 450 persons worked for Bell South Advertising and Publishing Company (BAPCO) was uninhabitable, without electricity or air conditioning; this was August, in South Florida. And 80 percent of the employees working in that building had either lost their homes or sustained severe damage. Imagine the difficulty of getting this workforce back on the job.

Transportation was difficult, with downed trees, stoplights out and street signs gone. Phones were dead, leaving few options for finding people other than physically going to their homes. We set up a networking system where employees would report on the known status of other employees—many unwilling to leave their homes for fear of looting. Managers and selected employees were dispatched to look for those on whom we had no information.

BAPCO employees were taken supplies, and offered housing. We knew no employees would come to work until they had a stable (even if temporary) place to live. So early steps were taken to secure housing for employees, even before everyone was accounted for. Additionally, BAPCO made food, childcare, supplies and even cash available to employees at their building. The word spread and many previously unaccounted for employees came in for assistance. This helped us account for everyone in record time.

Depending on the size and scope of the crisis, you may recognize that you need help in making order out of chaos. Perhaps between your crisis team and your humanitarian team, you still cannot handle every affected individual personally. Whoever is in charge on the ground needs to be directed to enlist reinforcements. This would ideally involve people who seem to be functioning reasonably well, and appear willing and able to respond to your instructions. This is a time when you need to enlist all resources available to you, with discretion.

Beyond the obvious benefit of additional hands in a time of need, putting others to work who are themselves reeling from what they've observed can help them gain a sense of composure and productiveness.

Who's Hurting?

Once you've attempted to account for your people and have enlisted some assistance, it's time to make an initial assessment of those who may be physically injured without realizing it, emotionally traumatized or otherwise deeply impacted. (The assumption is that those with serious physical injuries have been taken to hospitals.) This is an informal process that involves the step of simply asking those you see if they're aware of others who are having difficulty.

Obviously, a person dissolved in tears is suffering some degree of emotional distress. But it's often not that simple. Look as well for people who seem to be scattered, shocked, stunned, dazed or confused. Especially, look out for those who are withdrawn. Many people suffer quietly.

Ask employees and your enlisted helpers to be on the lookout for those who need help and to bring them to your attention. Professional crisis counseling needs to be provided. Compile a list of emotionally "at-risk" individuals. A timely response can make a difference that lasts a lifetime.

Gently encourage everyone to gather in a predetermined, comfortable space. Try not to use a large, open space like the company cafeteria, which can contribute to a feeling of vulnerability. Avoid one with many windows, to enhance a feeling of safety and also keep out inappropriately inquisitive reporters. As you escort them to the space, take care to shelter them from grisly images—like corpses being carried off, or bloodstained cubicles.

A common reaction among those who have been traumatized is to perseverate—to obsess—over a single lost object or issue, like a shoe or set of keys. The "small stuff" looms so large in their minds because it's all they can mentally process at the moment. Meet their needs. Find coffee, a tissue, a cell phone—whatever it takes to bring comfort.

Prepare for Family Members

While some members of your team are helping to keep people comfortable, others should prepare for the arrival of family members. Bad news travels fast, and kinfolk may make their way to your site more quickly than you can imagine. Establish a gathering place for arriving family members.

One strategy I recommend is to position sentries at the end of the driveway or entranceway to your facility. These are probably employees. If you have suffered fatalities, these official "greeters" should know the names of the dead. The strategy is simple—as cars or pedestrians come up, one of the sentries asks their affiliation with the company. If they are family members of someone who has died, a sentry will escort them to a private room where an appropriate manager will make the death notification.

Family members will want to see their loved ones *now!* Employees who are not injured should be connected with their loved ones as soon as possible in a family gathering area. Families of hospitalized employees would be escorted to another area of the building, where transportation to hospitals would be quickly provided, since people under duress are at risk of having auto accidents.

Do everything you can to connect family members with loved ones. Ideally, you will know who has been seriously injured and hospitalized. As emergency responders are transporting injured people, ask to what hospitals so that you can communicate this to the families. In incidents with mass casualties, it is likely that more than one hospital will be used. The last thing you want is to send frantic families on a chase from one emergency room to another.

You will be barraged with questions. What happened? Who or what was responsible? Who was nearby when the crisis hit? Was anyone killed? How many were injured?

Your duty is to be as informative as you can, delivering straight, truthful information. Don't beat around the bush, but don't speculate either. It's not up to you or other team members to offer a medical prognosis—remember that misinformation can lead to outrage. Dispel rumors if you can, and be forthcoming, though careful not to divulge information that will increase stress and anxiety.

Telling What They Know

If a crime was committed, the police will arrive to take statements. You will benefit the investigation by discouraging those affected from conversing among themselves about the events. The desire to commiserate and swap accounts is strong, but the police (and your own corporate investigators) will want to get the cleanest possible story from each witness—an account untainted by the recollections of others.

You could provide pads and pens for those who wish to make notes about what they saw before they talk with the police. This can aid the investigation, but sometimes traumatized people are simply too shaken to concentrate on writing.

De-escalation Meetings

Following police statements, your people will probably be eager to get away from the site, but don't let them go just yet. You need to hold "de-escalation meetings," where you take stock of what's happened, convey key information and assess their well-being.

Ideally, these meetings take place soon after the incident, before employees are sent home. Local management typically leads them. They can be conducted in large or small assemblies. If police are taking statements, wait until you have perhaps five or ten people before holding each session. If your facility operates more than one shift, or if people finish giving police statements at different times, you will want to conduct enough de-escalation meetings to adequately meet the needs of all impacted and help them get home sooner.

The de-escalation meeting is a discussion session that gives management an opportunity to:

- Provide current, appropriate information to employees and others following a traumatic incident
- Stabilize and calm employees from the emotions of the traumatic incident
- Educate those affected regarding potential stress reactions and symptoms
- Collect information
- Dispel rumors
- Inform employees about what will happen the next day back at work

De-escalation Meeting Content

The essential topics to cover during a de-escalation session include the following:

1. **Acknowledge the significance of the crisis** with words like, "We are all deeply saddened and shocked . . ."
2. **Reconstruct the facts to the degree possible.** Elicit input from those with different perspectives or accurate information.
3. **Advise everyone *not* to talk to the media.** Explain that members of the press may be waiting with microphones in hand outside the building or even outside the homes of those affected. Those who have never experienced the onslaught of the press may feel compelled or required to answer questions asked (or shouted!) to them. But employees need to realize how easily their words can be twisted out of context; few will have an understanding of potential liability and reputation issues for your organization. So they should be encouraged not to talk. Make sure they understand that company representatives will make official statements and that there is no need for individuals to talk.

Rationale for employees not talking to the media:

(While anyone has the right to talk to the media . . .)

- The wrong statement to the media can harm your coworkers, the company and others involved.

- The media are looking for the most emotional and controversial thing any employee will say or do.

- They will take what employees say out of context, and many times misquote it.

- Company personnel are typically shocked and stunned following traumatic incidents and not prepared to make public statements.

- Company personnel cannot predict what will be asked and will lack thought-out responses.

- If any employee insists on talking to the media, they should understand that they may not make any statement regarding company policy, or speak in any way on the company's behalf.

- It is best to allow people who are trained and prepared to speak to the media.

- Company personnel do not even need to tell media whom to contact. Tell your people, "If you are approached by the media, simply wave them off and don't let them engage you."

4. **Discuss expected reactions**. Tell people to expect anxiety and adrenaline reactions, loss of appetite, sleep disturbance, intrusive thoughts and concentration difficulties. Let employees know these reactions are normal and to be expected by most everyone.

5. **If possible, instruct everyone to come to work on the next workday.** Explain that this will not be a normal workday and that a management-led meeting will take place soon after they arrive. They will be briefed on the latest information about the situation. If your facility has been damaged and you don't yet know where the meeting will be held, let everyone know how they will be notified. Tell them, "It will be best for everyone if we can all work through our reactions together, instead of isolating at home." Promising up-to-date information is the best way to get everyone to attend.

6. **Ask if there are questions.** Even if the silence is slightly awkward, be patient—there may be important questions.

7. **Establish a buddy system.** Following severe situations, especially if surviving employees witnessed deaths or felt their lives threat-

ened, assign each person a buddy and ask that they make "meaningful contact" with each other by phone for the next few days. Concerns about buddies should be reported to a designated person so help can be offered.

8. **Arrange transportation** for anyone who requests it or appears too distraught to drive safely. Don't underestimate the power of distraction; even those who believe they're fine may find themselves shaking, confused or simply too upset to safely drive.

9. **Supervisors and local managers** should be advised to come early the following day to be briefed prior to employee arrivals.

10. **Remain afterward** to speak with anyone who still has questions more comfortably asked one-on-one.

TWELVE CONSIDERATIONS FOR ACHIEVING "ORDER"

1. Know where you want to go before you start taking action.
2. Communication to and from affected audiences is vital.
3. Management needs to be visible.
4. The early bird gets the worm. Identify and enact solutions as soon as possible.
5. Secure the incident site and establish a sense of safety.
6. Protect affected individuals from unwanted outsiders and influences.
7. Give direction regarding what people should do in the near term.
8. Utilize *all* the resources available to you, inside and outside your organization, to enhance a sense of order.
9. Anticipate what could escalate and take actions to prevent it.
10. Identify the true nature of your crisis and come up with answers.
11. Tell the truth and take appropriate responsibility.
12. Establish a recovery system that involves *all* impacted employees.

Creating order out of chaos is not a definitive process—as if one moment there's chaos, and the next moment resolution. Rather, it's an evolutionary process that includes both the humanitarian component and the content side of the crisis.

In the next chapter, we will look at additional considerations and guidelines to manage the crisis response during the first day of the incident.

Quick Use Response Guide

CHAPTER 6: CREATING ORDER OUT OF CHAOS

- Have you provided for the administering of emotional first aid including:
  - ○ Accounting for everyone
  - ○ Enlisting available individuals to help
  - ○ Making contact with victims and assisting them with immediate needs
  - ○ Sharing available information with them
  - ○ Preparing for the arrival of family members
  - ○ Making special arrangements to greet and address families of those who have died or are hospitalized
  - ○ Protecting family members from the media
  - ○ Gathering impacted people in a comfortable, non-threatening space
  - ○ Arranging to reunite family members with their loved ones as soon as possible
  - ○ Helping employees following statements to police?
- Have you planned for employee de-escalation meetings that:
  - ○ Stabilize those traumatized
  - ○ Establish accurate information
  - ○ Inform people about plans for tomorrow?
- Have you referred to the twelve considerations for achieving order?

CHAPTER 7

Additional Day One
Guidelines and Considerations

Crisis response is not linear, with sequential events that follow neatly and chronologically. The opposite is true. Many things are happening at once. The image of overlapping concentric circles may be a useful way to visualize the distinct, yet intersecting events and responses typical of day one and beyond.

In this chapter, we'll take a time-out, just as your Crisis Management Team should be taking periodic time-outs to coordinate efforts and gain perspective. We'll review a generic checklist of issues to be considered. This is a "go-to" chapter, meaning that it is an annotated list you can return to as needed to help assure that you are, in fact, covering your bases.

The focus is on day one CMT activity and assuring that you are doing all you can to keep those plates spinning simultaneously in the air.

Taking Stock

Crisis management is a circular process. And it doesn't always make intuitive sense to people who operate in a patterned, linear way. The steps look like this:

- Information-gathering
- Situation assessment
- Decision-making
- Remedial action

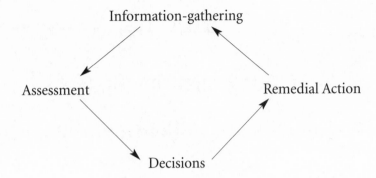

Let's take a walk through this checklist of considerations. We'll start with anticipated business impact.

A Tale of Two Traders

Consider what happened in the aftermath of the shootings by the day-trader Mark Barton in Atlanta, Georgia.

Barton terrorized two trading offices where he had been a losing trader, namely, the Atlanta office of All-Tech Investment Group, and Momentum across the street. Barton first shot eight, killing four at Momentum, then ran across the street and shot fourteen at All-Tech where he killed five. Essentially the same event at the same time, but the companies responded very differently. Corporate management from All-Tech reached a crisis consultant hours after the shooting, to assist with the aftermath of the traumatic events.

The consultant urged All-Tech decision-makers to carefully manage their humanitarian response. In this case, that included day one discussions and planning with top brass to remain open and gather the remaining All-Tech employees. On the next workday it meant a group stress debriefing for what turned out to be a room full of day-traders (All-Tech customers), which the crisis management consultant led.

Quickly, management had replaced the blood-soaked carpeting, shattered computers and other obvious signs of terror. By the next workday the physical space was essentially ready again for business.

Before the debriefing session, many day-traders came to the shooting site obviously dazed. No one was considering the stock market.

The consultant began by simply asking everyone to sit down. With a few probing questions, those affected were eager to tell their stories, surrounded by others who had been through the same nightmare. They exchanged gruesome recollections and mind-numbing fear as they crouched under furniture or ran to avoid Barton's wrath.

After about an hour of sharing collective experiences, one of the traders turned away from the circle and quietly rolled his chair over to his computer terminal. He began intermittent gazing at the screen and then tuning back into what was being said in the group discussion. An individual who had witnessed horrific events only hours before responded by doing the most normal thing in the world for a day-trader—checking the progress of the market!

But only after he was able to identify his difficult reactions as normal was he able to refocus his attentions on finances. Soon, the cloud of gloom was lifted enough that others began checking their computer screens. Were they over it? Not a chance. There would be (and still are for many) very difficult adjustments. But, All-Tech management provided the crisis leadership that allowed their customers to quickly begin recovering.

Losing Momentum

The posture adopted by All-Tech differed considerably from choices made by the leaders of Momentum, the first of Mark Barton's stops on that fateful day.

The firm accepted ill-equipped, yet free, crisis counseling offered by Atlanta's mayor. Intuitively, management decided to remain closed for some time to allow people and the company to cope. "Some time" morphed into about six weeks, an eternity to a business as entrenched in the moment as day-trading.

Momentum reopened, but, as you may already have guessed, the doors closed before long. For lack of a better term, the firm had lost its "momentum" among customers. The closing—precipitated by day one decisions—gave the business the aura of an unprepared, injured enterprise that would never regain its formerly robust character.

No reputable expert would counsel a business to act as if a life-changing crisis had not happened. But it can be unnecessarily detrimental to individuals and to a business to lie dormant too long in the wake of traumatic events.

Crisis Management Team Checklist

Let's turn now to the Day One Crisis Management Team Checklist. Feel free to supplement this generic list with concerns specific to your situation. (A supplemental listing of actions and considerations for specific crises is provided in the last chapter of this book.)

- **Work continuation.** Whether to close, what parts of the business, and for how long are complex questions with big implications. Sometimes, there is work that must go on. Employees understand that there are some areas of the organization that must remain operative.

  For example, a power company had an employee shooting in the payroll department right before payroll was due. While the supervisor and manager of the department were shot and the perpetrator killed herself, 15,000 others still needed their checks. Here the job was to balance getting payroll out while compassionately assisting those who witnessed the shootings.

  As a general rule, you must meet people needs before back-to-work needs. Otherwise you risk creating an atmosphere of resentment.

- **Financial considerations.** These can be staggering. Many times in the chaos of crisis response, there is little or no tracking of expenditures incurred. The surprise and second-guessing then comes at the end. CMI has developed the humanitarian response side of a software program that provides real-time tracking of expenditures during crisis management. This software complies with the Incident Command System (ICS) that is mandated by the Coast Guard following oil and gas incidents at sea. No matter how sophisticated or rudimentary your system, keeping track of expenses during crisis management should be a high priority. Still, crisis response is typically a time to be forthcoming with supportive resources.

- **Legal concerns.** Liability will be one of the first, and potentially most complex legal issues. Do you need specialized legal help to assure that you're minimizing legal risk? It may also be necessary to hire any consultants *through* your legal counsel, rather than directly. This can provide a layer of legal protection by safeguarding information under attorney-client privilege.

   In my crisis management experience, I have observed two types of attorneys—the *can do* and the *can't do* variety. The *can't do* lawyers have an easy answer for almost every request: "No." That response is usually based on an overly conservative concern for the kind of fallout a particular action might have on the attorney's ability to defend it. It also reflects a strong self-preservation instinct. Look for attorneys who will recognize legal concerns, but work with you in taking the crisis management actions that are needed by saying, "There are some legal hurdles to consider, but let's get you over them." Management, not attorneys, should drive crisis response. Your legal representatives are key partners in your effort to recover from a crisis; they shouldn't make your job more difficult.

- **Employee access.** Some employees will shy away from the site, while others will want—and may even need—to return to the scene to help them mentally grasp the incident. If employees will be allowed back in soon, the environment should be clean, but not necessarily oversanitized.

   A company that had experienced a workplace shooting in Miami knew that some employees were interested in seeing the incident site. But when I arrived prior to employees return to work, I saw a picture hung on the wall about eight feet high, up in a corner in order to cover a bullet hole from the previous day's shooting. I recommended it be taken down so employees who wanted to see the scene could get a "feel" for what had happened. Furniture remained overturned during the first day back. Only the blood-soaked carpet and wallpaper were ripped out.

   There are other decisions to make about the workspace, desk or office of deceased workers. One possibility is to remove any sensitive business materials and files. Leave personal items, like pictures of the family. Then announce that any employee can informally visit the deceased person's workspace to say last good-byes. This typically remains in place until the funeral.

- **Management outreach.** Clarify what support the company will *and will not* offer. Will the company fly in relatives of dead or seriously injured employees? The balancing act with families is to accommodate, while not be taken advantage of. One commercial airline reportedly found a bill for a Rolex watch that a hospitalized passenger's relative charged to his hotel room. In this instance, the airline decided to pay the bill and be taken advantage of, rather than fight the issue. Although there may be some abuses, it is best to be forthcoming regarding reasonable requests. This is not a time to be penny-wise and pound-foolish.

- **Media messages.** The messages you wish to convey should be thoughtfully crafted, and recrafted as needed, by your PR/communications director, the Crisis Management Team and other company leaders. At a minimum, you should agree on the main messages that you want to get out through your communicators. Determine the deadlines reporters must meet, in order to get timely coverage of your side of the story. Stay in the driver's seat by regularly updating the press, giving the media meaningful information and monitoring coverage.

  If you bring on outside PR assistance, choose carefully. The profession has many sub-specialties. Expertise at investor relations does not necessarily translate to the area of emergency response. You want someone who knows your industry, your media market and how to lead your communications efforts through chaotic times. Your PR professional should lend valuable counsel about matching the message to the various target audiences.

- **Role of labor.** The quality of your relationship with labor before the crisis will likely define the quality of your post-event interaction. Many companies have found that union stewards and other leaders can contribute significantly to crisis management, as team members, family representatives and in other ways appropriate to your organizational culture.

- **Controlling blame and outrage.** A forthright approach to communicating about your crisis can help defuse outrage. Usually, outrage

emanates from beliefs that the cause for the incident was intentional, foreseeable, avoidable or unjust. Possibilities for addressing
outrage include giving accurate information about the incident,
educating the public about the hazard, taking appropriate responsibility for the occurrence and/or response, showing heartfelt caring and compassion, and taking resolute actions to assure it will
never happen again.

- **Mitigating further escalation.** Every action causes a reaction. It is
important to consider the chain of events that could play out in the
aftermath of your crisis. Play the "If . . . then" and "What if . . ."
games to anticipate what could happen in the foreseeable future.
Only when you accurately anticipate the various repercussions of
your situation can you adequately prepare for, rather than react to,
potential escalations. Take intermittent time-outs to ponder where
this situation may be headed. Think also about the long-term consequences of the actions you are taking today.

- **Time-off policy.** It may appear counterintuitive, but it's often better for workers to get back to work soon after traumatic incidents.
Balanced approaches of remaining productive and pampering one-
self will usually accelerate personal and corporate recovery. Management should understand employees will initially not be 100
percent productive. Acknowledge this and show compassion as you
evolve back into full productivity over time.

- **Funeral/memorial service attendance policy.** Will employees be
given time off to attend funeral services of coworkers killed on
the job? Will it be paid or unpaid leave? Is there a need for a
company-sponsored memorial service? This may be especially
important if a deceased coworker's funeral is back home in a dis-
tant state.

- **Shrines and memorials.** Beware of employees' and families' de-
sires to establish shrines and memorials on your property. These
can transform your lobby into something resembling a cemetery
over time. Many companies are willing to place a memorial
wreath of flowers in the lobby until the time of the funeral. I usually recommend the planting of a tree on company property. If
you do this, make every effort to see that the tree doesn't die pre-
maturely.

- **Investigation and prevention plan.** As a part of your response actions, a team of individuals should be assigned the task of investigating the incident and developing a plan to prevent reoccurrences.

The following are also part of a day one checklist, and have been discussed in depth in previous chapters.

- Keeping a phone log
- Controlling outgoing information and rumors
- Securing, cleaning up and repairing the site of the incident
- Gathering and verifying information about the incident
- Notifying next-of-kin of anyone hurt or killed
- Sending family assistance representatives to support kin
- Mental health assistance for traumatized people
- Others as you deem appropriate

Ten Questions to Assess Your Decisions and Actions

Many of our client companies have found useful a ten-question checklist that helps them gauge the appropriateness of Crisis Management Team decisions and actions. Consider these—and feel free to alter them to suit your organization. You may wish to keep these questions posted in the Crisis Command Center. For every crisis response action, ask:

1. Does it protect company assets, shareholder value, reputation and the well-being of those affected?
2. Does it consider broad, long-term implications?
3. Will it accelerate the recovery process?
4. Have contingencies been carefully appraised, and are reasonable contingency plans in place?
5. Have alternative courses of action been considered?
6. Are legal concerns adequately covered?
7. Is it based on substantiated facts?
8. Is it based on sound business practice?

9. Are adequate monitoring and quality assurance measures in place to assure it is working?

10. Would we feel comfortable defending this decision or action if it ended up on the front page of the newspaper?

In the next chapter, we will turn our attention to the families of those seriously injured or killed. We will take an in-depth look at how to compassionately address family needs and avoid common pitfalls.

Quick Use Response Guide

CHAPTER 7: ADDITIONAL DAY ONE GUIDELINES AND CONSIDERATIONS

Have you taken day one steps and actions in areas including:

- Security access controls
- Phone log
- Outgoing communications
- Incoming communications
- Next-of-kin notification
- Family assistance representatives
- Professional crisis consultation and counseling
- Work continuation
- Financial considerations
- Legal concerns
- Incident site cleanup and repairs
- Employee access
- Management outreach
- Media messages
- Role of labor
- Controlling blame and outrage
- Mitigating further escalation
- Planning for first day back
- Funeral/memorial service attendance policy
- Time-off policy

- Shrines and memorials
- Rumor control
- Investigation and prevention plan

Has your team considered the ten Questions to Assess Your Decisions and Actions?

1. Does it protect company assets, shareholder value, reputation and the well-being of those affected?
2. Does it consider broad, long-term implications?
3. Will it accelerate the recovery process?
4. Have contingencies been carefully appraised, and are reasonable contingency plans in place?
5. Have alternative courses of action been considered?
6. Are legal concerns adequately covered?
7. Is it based on substantiated facts?
8. Is it based on sound business practice?
9. Are adequate monitoring and quality assurance measures in place to assure it is working?
10. Would we feel comfortable defending this decision or action if it ended up on the front page of the newspaper?

CHAPTER 8

Addressing the Families of Casualties

Few duties are more difficult than knocking on the door of the home of a young mother whose husband has been killed in an industrial accident.

Whether you meet grieving families in makeshift morgues, at four–star hotels or in remote fields strewn with airplane fragments the same principles apply. This chapter will lay out those principles, addressing the following topics:

- Assisting arriving family members
- The role of family representatives
- Visits by senior management

Although the techniques outlined can make a significant difference in your interactions with impacted family members, much of your success will derive from your initial approach. Try to remember how it felt when others used the right (or wrong) approach during your own times of need.

Before you go on such a visit, spend a few minutes visualizing what these individuals are facing. What mix of emotions are they most likely experiencing? What information do you anticipate they will need?

Beware of Intruders

In Chapter Six, I touched on the post-event arrival of family members, and outlined key points, including the need for a sentry at your entrances. One purpose is to separate out the families of fatalities. They should be greeted with proper concern and kindness and led to a separate location. The greeter should not, however, share the bad news; this should be done by appropriate management or team leaders.

Another equally important reason to meet and escort all arriving family members is to keep them from the sensation-crazed press. I have no personal prejudice against the media; in fact, they have been very good to our organization. But as a crisis management consultant I have seen too many insensitive actions justified in the name of "getting the story."

An explosion at a steel company with which we worked caught an employee in a pool of molten steel that flowed onto the floor. His coworkers could only watch, until the steel had cooled; he died of his injuries a few days later. Families heard of the explosion and rushed to the plant, unaware of the identity of the victim.

Unfortunately, the media got there first. As each family group made its way to the plant entrance, "enterprising" reporters jumped in front of them, stuck a microphone in their faces and asked their reactions. These poor souls had no idea if their loved one was involved. The offending television station used the most emotional clips of this ill-gotten "story" on the evening news. It is in the best interest of your organization and the family members, as well, to protect them from such encroachments.

"Legal" Offenders

As stricken kin make their way to your facility, members of the press aren't the only ones they need to look out for. An ambulance-chasing lawyer can rival—and even exceed—the zeal of a story-seeking journalist.

Remember the Coca-Cola Enterprises bottling plant in McAllen, Texas, whose delivery truck rammed into a school bus? A migrant farm worker family arrived at the site. They had been late in learning about the crash and rushed over to the accident scene to find out if their child had been a victim. A plaintiff's attorney lying in wait intercepted the family, and promised them a ride to the hospital.

En route to the hospital, this smarmy lawyer stopped at his office where he presented the family a contract for legal services, even though his action was against state law. Their English was marginal, their understanding of the documents was vague and their desire to see the child was overwhelming. They unwittingly signed the documents.

If the incident occurs on your site, you have the right to keep the media and other outsiders off your property. Ask law enforcement to assist you in this effort. If necessary, utilize your own personnel, bring in off-duty police, or whatever it takes to keep predators away from family members and others, at your site or, possibly, at their own homes.

Bringing People Together

I recommend you assign employees to meet arriving family members and bring them to a designated gathering place.

Use an alternative location for employees and family members to assemble if fires, spewing toxins or other hazards have rendered your workplace uninhabitable. Hotels are common alternatives and provide a number of advantages, including plenty of meeting space, parking and the availability of private rooms and communications resources.

Another choice is a community center or church. The latter offers many benefits, not the least of which is the sense of solace that a house of worship brings, whatever the religion or denomination. Consider the possibility that any gathering place you identify might have to serve as a family meeting place for days, especially in a mass casualty situation as was the case with one church following the Oklahoma City bombing.

Assigning Family Representatives

It's been demonstrated time and again that the comfort and support of others is one of the best means to speed the emotional recovery of relatives of a crisis victim. Family representatives—specially trained individuals who are assigned to a victim's family—can play a critical role in compassionately reaching out to families. Their job is an important and difficult one.

Contact should be initiated with the family as soon as possible. Two representatives, ideally a man and a woman, would be assigned to the family of every individual seriously injured or killed. The teams should be trained in advance and should be aware of relevant company policies and the scope of assistance available.

Be sensitive to any language or cultural issues. Make sure each family's representatives speak their language, or that a skilled translator is present who might also know their customs.

Family representatives:

- Serve as the primary point of contact between impacted families and the company
- Assist with emergency travel and other arrangements for remote family members
- Help with hospital liaison and funeral arrangements if necessary
- Respond to any type of reasonable assistance the family may need

They also serve as a communication resource between the family and the company. Part of their job includes communicating needs and concerns to the Crisis Management or Humanitarian Response Teams. Authorization for special requests will also be conveyed through the representatives.

The representatives' ability to act in a sensitive, caring and effective manner will not only help relatives cope, but will improve the relationship between the family and the company.

A Word of Caution

Be cautious of the emotional attachments that can result. As assignments are made, be careful not to assign someone who may identify "too closely" with a particular family or its problems.

As American Airlines responded to a 1994 crash in Indiana, a family representative asked me to help with a man whose wife, the mother of their children, had died in the crash. The woman and her husband had been the parents of a seven-year-old son, the age of my daughter at the time. Watching this child begin to grieve, including writing a letter to his mom and burning it in the fireplace so she would get it in heaven, was extremely difficult for me. The youngster reminded me of my own child, and it hit me very hard. This made it difficult for me to let go emotionally when my work was done with this family.

That Knock on the Door

Following initial death notification, it's likely that family representatives (not the same individuals who gave the notification) will meet relatives at the victims' homes. They should call in advance. If possible, do not park in or block the driveway. Upon arriving, they should identify themselves as representatives of the company, shake hands, then ask to come in, speaking to each member of the family, including any children present. Get names ahead of time, if possible.

In such situations, it's generally a good idea to look for a dining room or kitchen chair and say that you prefer a hard chair. This keeps you from inadvertently sitting in the victim's favorite spot. It also permits you to place the chair where you want it, with access to everyone in the room.

The representative should express concern and intent with words like: *"I first want to express my shock and heartfelt sadness over what has happened. I am here to help you with any problems, or needs you may have. I will serve as a source of information and communication between your family and the company."*

The goal at this session is to elicit conversation. Company representatives should talk less and listen more, using expressions like, *"Please tell me about any needs you may have,"* *"What are your concerns at this time?"* *"What needs to be done right away?"* and *"Do I understand clearly that you would like . . . ?"*

Among phrases to avoid:
"How are you doing?"
"I know exactly how you feel."
"It could have been worse, you know."
"Everything happens for a reason."
"It's God's will."

More appropriate choices are:
"I'm here to help."
"I can only imagine how difficult this must be for you."
"I'll look into that and get right back to you."

No matter how carefully the phrases are chosen, it's likely that family members will react with some combination of denial, numbness, anger, remorse, shock, confusion, anxiety and grief. They do want accurate information and family reps should be prepared with answers to the "what happened and why" questions.

Other Locations, Same Message

Family assistance personnel may also make their initial visits at a hospital. It is not always necessary to make an appointment before hospital visits, but you may want to phone ahead to confirm that it is a good time to meet. Considerations for the initial meeting include:

- Before meeting the family, ask a hospital staff member to help you arrange for a private place to meet. Preferably, the hospital will have family meeting rooms. Check the room out before meeting the family.
- If family members are in a large waiting room with other people, ask the nurse to quietly point out those you are looking for.
- If you are entering a patient room, knock softly, wait and then enter slowly.
- Quietly introduce yourself and confirm that you are speaking with the proper person(s). Shake hands. Use discretion about a gentle touch on the shoulder or other appropriate gesture. Suggest that you all meet "to discuss some issues" in a private place you have arranged. In a patient room, use discretion whether to talk there or go to a private place.
- Express heartfelt sorrow and clarify your role, with the same questions and statements suggested above.
- If extended family members wish to participate in the discussion, welcome them and listen to their input. They can be helpful in interpreting the needs of the immediate family, but they may also express the most anger.
- Have a list of questions you want to ask. Also, list out possible items or services you could provide, such as cell phones, rental cars, hotel or travel arrangements, errands, child care, etc.
- Use active listening techniques, as in: *"I hear you saying you're concerned about . . . is that right?"*
- Make sure the family knows how to be in touch with you.

Similarly, if you are meeting with family members at the airport, find a private place to do so. A simple sign to identify the family you're looking for eliminates awkwardness. If members of the press are present, put first names and last initial only on the sign. Don't wear anything that displays your corporate name or logo. Lead family members away from the area and protect them from intrusive press and media representatives.

If your initial encounter with the family takes place at a hotel, arrange first for a private meeting place.

An Emotional Roller Coaster

The depth of the stress on family members who have recently learned that their loved one is critically injured or dead is unfathomable. The shock and anxiety may be accompanied by an immobilizing numbed state. A refusal to believe what they have heard may be coupled with an urgent need to learn more and take action. The combinations of colliding, even conflicting emotions and needs can be confusing.

It's also true that different crisis situations elicit different reactions. An airline crash, or other man-made disaster, typically leads to more anger, resentment and culpability than natural disasters, where there are "no persons" to blame. Multiple reactions can include exhaustion, guilt, an inability to eat or sleep, trouble concentrating and mood swings.

Relatives should be encouraged to express their concerns and issues. Family reps may wish to tell them that emotional reactions typically come in waves—they may feel overwhelmed at one moment, and rather numb the next.

Well-meaning family representatives who do everything "by the book" should not be surprised if they are the targets of some anger and outrage. They must avoid taking it personally. And they should avoid the temptation to take on inappropriate roles, such as medical advisor or psychologist. Remember the limits of the family rep's role. They should assess needs, assist with tasks and arrangements, and serve as a conduit of communication to and from the company. Counseling issues should be referred to crisis-experienced mental health professionals.

If issues of getting an attorney come up, the family rep should take the neutral position that the family should do whatever they feel is appropriate.

The family representative's role is to genuinely assist with family members' needs without any appearances of ulterior motives.

Senior Management Visits

Between twelve and forty-eight hours after a serious injury or death, a senior manager should visit the families of serious and fatal casualties. Beforehand, a family representative or member of the Humanitarian Response Team should prepare a short "backgrounder" sheet with information needed to greet the family appropriately. This may include the names and pertinent facts about individual family members, their requests and needs, and personal information about the victim.

The manager may wish to have as many as two people accompany him or her. Perhaps a crisis mental health specialist and a human resources manager who is knowledgeable about benefits. If the family rep has established a good rapport with the family, it may be good to have them there too, but do not overwhelm the family with too many visitors. Everyone who goes should have a designated role, or else they should not attend during the senior management visit. The same guidelines presented above, such as making a proper introduction and expressing heartfelt condolences, apply to senior managers.

But then what? After those initial sentiments are conveyed, an uncomfortable silence often descends upon the room. The key is to keep conversation flowing.

For example, the executive might ask a spouse or parent, "*Where were you when you first heard about the incident?*" Keep things going with questions like, "*So what happened between the time you got the phone call and when you arrived at the hospital?*" Without prying, the executive is giving the distinct impression of caring about the people involved. Another strategy is to say, "*Tell me a little about Charlie. What was he like at home?*" It would also be good if the senior manager or other company person in attendance could relate some interesting facts about the victim at work or messages from coworkers.

I've seen this approach work time and again. Families want *and need* to talk about what they have been through and about their loved ones. It happened when I accompanied the founder of a pizza chain to a hospital. He had the unenviable task of meeting with the parents of a young man, a delivery driver who had been seriously injured as he attempted to help a stranded motorist.

I could actually see the parents' comfort level rise as they spoke lovingly about their son, answering the company president's polite, gentle questions. The meeting ended with hugs. And the grateful parents wrote the executive a letter, thanking him warmly for his expression of concern.

Time to Disengage

Disengagement can be the hardest part for family representatives, who, by nature, are caring people. There will never be a time when they have done "everything possible" for the family. But there will be a moment when it is time to separate.

The expectation of eventual disengagement should begin as early as the initial meeting. It would be good for the family rep to describe the scope of involvement as being *"over the next few days or weeks."* Make clear that other, longer-term assistance will be provided as needed, through helping referrals and community resources.

It is time to disengage when:

- The scope of initial assistance is completed and the family has an adequate support system of longer-term helpers
- Management and the family rep agree that it is time to discontinue
- An attorney is retained and intervenes
- The family declines further assistance
- Other signs indicate the time is right

When the interaction with the family has formally ended, family representatives need to go through a formal disengagement process, as well. This should include a debriefing with other family representatives about the experience and recognition that although holiday cards may be exchanged, the relationship has served its purpose and is over. It's easier said than done.

Everyone has heard stories of heroes (and family reps can be just that in many cases) who suffer after their mission of mercy is complete. A poignant example is the story of Baby Jessica in Midland, Texas. In 1987, rescuers worked for fifty-eight hours to free the eighteen-month-old who had fallen into a twenty-foot hole. One of the paramedics who hoisted her out became an instant celebrity. But celebrity waned and he eventually took his own life; according to his brother, the stress of the experience was a cause of his suicide.

This extreme example underscores the necessity of special attention for those who care for others. Interacting with emotionally wounded, hurting family members is an enormously important part of crisis management. It promises considerable rewards, but it carries risks that should not be ignored.

Quick Use Response Guide

CHAPTER 8: ADDRESSING THE
FAMILIES OF CASUALTIES

- Are you prepared for family interactions including:
  ○ Assisting arriving family members
  ○ Protecting families from the media and interfering attorneys
  ○ Techniques for meeting families at home, at the hospital or other public places or over the phone?
- Has a trained team of employees been assigned to serve as family representatives?
- Has a manual of guidelines been provided to family representatives?
- Have you prepared senior managers for visits with family members?
- Have you established disengagement policies and procedures for family reps?

CHAPTER 9

Crisis Communications

As a manager in the business world, you surely know the crucial importance of good, effective communication. No doubt you have worked hard to develop the particular skills it requires, like expressing yourself with precision and economy, and listening well.

During a crisis, you will need to rely on all those same skills. But just as a moment of disaster is different from any routine time, crisis communications are far different from normal, day-to-day communications. In a crisis, everything is more emotionally charged, and moving at top velocity. You and your actions are unusually—perhaps uncomfortably—visible. Everything is said and heard in a context of rumors, potential misunderstandings and high scrutiny.

Ground Rules for Effective Crisis Communications

From the very moment you begin a crisis response:

- Employ the communications technique of the military and the airline industry: Repeat back what you hear. If someone repeats information incorrectly, it will be recognized immediately, and the dangers of inaccuracy and misunderstandings avoided.
- Orient all communications toward action. Effective crisis response is not passive. It is what you *do* that is most important. Actions need to be well thought out, but all communications and discussions should be focused; ask, "What do we do with this informa-

tion?" When information comes to you that does not call for action, move on. Let the pontificators sound off on their own time. Crisis Management Teams don't have that luxury.

Giving Information Out: Keeping Control of the Message

Staying in control of your outgoing message means being clear about both how it is delivered, and what it contains.

Who should do the talking? Decide who will be your spokespersons, brief them on the agreed-upon messages and prepare them for each appearance they will make. Spokespersons can be individuals from the company's communications department, senior management, site management, legal department, those with applicable technical knowledge, outside specialists and experts, or others. Beware of divergent or contradictory statements being made from within your organization. All communications should be funneled through a gatekeeper for accuracy and consistency, as well as conformity to your response strategy, before being released. If your organization is international, you may require special coordination of the timing and information that reaches the investment communities in affected countries.

To whom are you speaking? You should identify each audience that needs communication from you. Establish and maintain a schedule for both initial and ongoing communications to each of them. They can include:

- Your employees, including staff management
- Employees' families
- Senior management
- The board of directors
- Your business partners
- The investment community
- Insurance representatives
- Your suppliers, distributors and franchisees
- Your customers
- Government and law enforcement officials

- Industry activist groups
- Media representatives
- Unions
- Affected community members
- Retained technical experts
- And don't neglect your own family, who will want to know how you are

How should the parameters of the crisis be defined? It is up to you to identify the extent of what has happened. Doing so quickly and decisively can go a long way toward preventing counterproductive speculation and sensationalism. Quarantine what is affected from what is not affected. This is called "isolating the crisis."

For example, if you determine that fire has destroyed your Northwestern distribution center, you will be able to make that statement while adding, "All our other distribution centers are fully functional and will pick up the slack for timely deliveries to our customers."

What needs to be communicated immediately? Most likely, you will make an initial statement, or series of them, even before solutions to the problem have been set in motion. Usually these are "holding" statements, in which a company official reports what is known and verified, and makes clear that further investigations are underway and responses set to go. As a general rule, come up with solutions to realistic and perceived problems and communicate those solutions to affected audiences as soon as possible.

What are the main things to say? Determine your main messages for both external and internal audiences and then prepare consistent answers to the questions you can anticipate from each group.

If people have been traumatized physically or emotionally, always begin your statements with a heartfelt concern for the well-being of everyone impacted. In this, be careful not to leave out any affected groups, even those indirectly affected, such as distressed but uninjured employees, families of casualties or members of your local community who may have felt threatened.

Sometimes managers are reluctant to express regret for damage or injuries that have occurred, fearing that to do so might encourage people to consider the company liable. But it is certainly possible to express sympathy and regret without taking blame or responsibility. Indeed, doing so might ultimately diminish your exposure to lawsuits, by defusing the sense of outrage that helps to generate them.

In your communications, strive to isolate the crisis to the smallest scope that can contain it, to keep it from escalating into or being perceived as a company-wide issue. If you don't know the answer to "why the incident happened," inform concerned audiences that investigations are underway.

Do not admit negligence or liability. Make no promises concerning financial compensation or repair of damages unless fully agreed upon as a solution by your management team. Put the situation into perspective by noting, for example, your company's outstanding safety record or leadership in community affairs; the one in a million chance this incident could happen; how it is isolated to only a small portion of the company; how the company itself may have been victimized; and the like.

Honesty—the Best Policy—Does Not Mean Saying Everything

Dishonesty can cause a crisis to escalate faster than any other single mistake. Following catastrophes, the media, attorneys, government officials and the public are naturally looking for scandal, negligence and scapegoats. Any evidence, or even hint, that you are being dishonest or withholding important information can be expected to elicit immediate and uncomfortable scrutiny from them all.

However, you don't have to say everything you know in your outgoing communications. Sometimes there is information that you may appropriately choose not to publicly divulge. It is rarely a good idea, for example, in the immediate aftermath of the crisis to discuss issues of responsibility and cause. You will rarely know the entire story yourself at this point, and there is plenty of time once things settle down for investigations both by yourselves and by any interested outside parties. You also want to avoid any statement that could be construed as the basis of a liability action.

However, beware of giving an appearance of deception by omission, if it should be learned that you are holding back important information. Discuss both the pros and cons of how much to tell. Consider, for example, what impact there could be if the information is disclosed willingly by you—or alternatively, is uncovered by a reporter.

Communication Is a Human Art

In this book I emphasize the too-often ignored human impacts of crisis. At a time of crisis, your employees and other people associated with your company can be your allies—or your enemies. They have inside information. And what they hear from you, and how they hear it, can make a difference. Make sure the people in and close to your organization are given accurate and timely information. Outrage has been the observed result time and again, when employees obtained information from sources outside the company, instead of from management.

Your employees spend one third of each workday with you. The company provides their livelihoods and a considerable part of their sense of self-identification. They will closely identify with any crisis that hits you, and feel affected, whether they are injured or not. The unenlightened company only pays attention to external constituencies at a time of crisis, and only addresses the immediate needs of those who might be injured. Wise management takes a more holistic view, supporting—and in turn being supported by—its work force.

Media Relations During a Crisis

If your crisis gets their attention, the media will put out a story, whether you participate or not. While you do not have control over reporters and editors, you can manage the information you give them, and have a great deal of influence on how you are presented.

When a crisis starts. Use prepared holding statements if the media contacts you before you are prepared to provide incident-specific statements. Holding statements can be prepared ahead of time and pre-approved by management for use in the early aftermath of any catastrophe. This will buy time until you can organize your response and draft messages specific to the event.

Advertising concerns. Consider whether you want to stop paid advertising for the time being. Could yesterday's ads be putting out a message that, in light of today's crisis, is suddenly inappropriate?

Tune in. Stay abreast of the evolving stories about your incident in the news media, by monitoring broadcasts. This can be a big job, and you might delegate others to handle it, freeing your team for other necessary tasks. Keep your management team informed about the coverage. Invariably, the media will publish misinformation. Remember that the media can serve as a source of information for you, too. Many times, reporters have provided vital, up-to-date information to the company during phone calls while they are in pursuit of additional information.

Watch what you say. Outgoing communications should be prepared in conjunction with legal counsel, your communications department, your management team and possibly law enforcement. Just as you do not want to say anything that could increase your liability or reputational damage, you do not want to jeopardize any possible criminal investigations.

Develop your message. Anticipate reporters' questions so that you will be prepared with answers you can control. Prior to press conferences, it is to your advantage to ask what they will want to know. Here are some typical questions you can expect to be asked.

- What happened? How bad is it? What is the extent of property damage, or injuries? What is the intensity and scope? Is there continuing danger?
- Why did it happen? How did it happen? Who is responsible? Do *you* feel responsible? Has this happened before? Are there any signs of impropriety?
- What is the company doing in response? How soon will the situation be under control?
- What is being done to keep it from happening again? How are you preparing to respond to future incidents?

Before a Press Conference or Interview

In planning for a press conference or media interview, decide on *specific points* you want to get across. Script and rehearse these messages. Even in an interview where your spokesperson may have to answer questions that are unexpected or that come in a surprising order, he or she should get those points into the response.

If people have been traumatized, begin by expressing compassion and genuine concern for all those affected. Say, "First, let me express my heartfelt sorrow for what happened . . ." Then keep your statements concise and factual. You don't want to appear wooden, but that does not mean you should let yourself speculate or be drawn. Be truthful, but don't overly elaborate. Remember, you don't have to tell everything you know. If questioning starts to get out of hand, you can conclude the conference by announcing that you will take just one more question, and then leave.

Working with the Press Corps

My experience is that reporters can be an excellent source of information in the aftermath of crises. You will benefit if you establish good relations and two-way communication with them.

Respect the professional needs of media people, like the deadlines they face. Inform them how often you will provide updated information, and stick to that schedule. Assure them that you will let them know as soon as possible if significant news breaks—and then do so. Do your best to accommodate requests made by the media and always treat them with respect. If the media is to be camped out at your location for the long haul, provide accommodations for them, such as access to food, water, toilets and shelter.

However, do not cede control of your message to them. Don't, for example, allow them to film your spokesperson with the company logo—or worse yet, your burning building—in the background. You hardly want this to be the main image people retain of the incident. Do not respond to media requests haphazardly or improvisationally. Take the initiative by organizing press conferences and providing press statements.

Beyond the News Media

Keep in mind that the news media are not the only information conduits you can utilize to give and receive vital information. In many crisis situations, you can make valuable use of communication methods like:

• Supervisor meetings with their employees
• Town hall meetings

- Phone trees
- Toll-free hotlines
- Surveys and questionnaires
- Paid advertising
- Lessons-learned debriefings
- Union meetings
- Bulletin boards
- Websites

Protect Your People from Media Intrusions

When a crisis hits, quickly inform all employees where to refer calls from frantic family members, media and others. Inform them that only appointed company spokespersons are authorized to speak to the media, regulators and other authorities.

To help manage intrusive calls, forward incoming calls for specified phones either to voice mail or to the appropriate person within the company. In some instances, you may want to instruct your people not to answer calls from unknown numbers, and instead to only take voice mails from such callers.

Remember that sometimes the media can serve as a resource in communicating with your employees, for example by broadcasting announcements regarding the temporary closing of a facility.

Refer to Chapter Six, where we discussed in depth the reasons why employees other than designated spokespeople should not talk to the media.

Ongoing and Long-term Communications

Sometimes a crisis extends over a considerable time. Here are some tips for managing media relations in such a situation.

- Utilize a single person to communicate with the media over the long haul.
- It is critical that this spokesperson be readily available to the media.
- Monitor the statements and reports of the media and take steps to correct any misinformation or misperceptions.

- Instruct all managers and other employees to remain courteous toward media people.
- While some reporters may be more favorable toward the company, be careful not to show obvious favoritism toward them. You certainly don't want to further irritate any reporters who are already negative toward you.

Remember to give communications to and from your Crisis Management Team the highest priority. They are the lifeblood of your effective crisis response.

Quick Use Response Guide

CHAPTER 9: CRISIS COMMUNICATIONS

- Have you employed the military's technique, repeating back what you hear?
- Have you oriented all communications toward action?
- Right at the start, have you asked the right questions?
  - What happened?
  - How bad is it?
  - Who can tell us more?
  - What else might happen?
  - Who or what is responsible for the incident?
  - What is being done so far in response?
  - How is the media involved?
- Have you decided who should do the talking, and channeled all communications through a gatekeeper?
- Have you considered all your potential audiences?
  - Your employees, including staff and management
  - Employees' families
  - Senior management
  - The board of directors
  - Your business partners
  - The investment community
  - Insurance representatives
  - Your suppliers, distributors and franchisees

- ○ Your customers
- ○ Government and law enforcement officials
- ○ Industry activist groups
- ○ Media representatives
- ○ Unions
- ○ The general community
- ○ Retained technical experts
- Have you defined the parameters of—or isolated—the crisis?
- Have you developed your messages for both external and internal audiences, and prepared consistent answers to the questions you can anticipate from each group?
  - ○ Have you discussed the pros and cons of how much to tell?
  - ○ Have you considered the emotional impact of the incident on your employees, and secured their support through quick communication?
- Have you prepared to manage your relations with the media?
  - ○ Have you prepared initial holding statements?
  - ○ Have you considered whether to suspend paid advertising?
  - ○ Are you monitoring news coverage of your incident?
  - ○ Have you prepared outgoing communications in conjunction with legal counsel, your communications department, your management team and possibly law enforcement?
  - ○ Have you anticipated, and asked for, reporters' questions in advance of any news conferences or interviews?
  - ○ Have you decided on *specific points* to get across in any statements to the media?
  - ○ Has your spokesperson rehearsed your message?
  - ○ Are you respecting the professional and personal needs of media people who are covering the story?
  - ○ Have you taken steps to protect your people from media intrusions?
- Have you considered other forums you can use for giving and receiving vital information?

CHAPTER 10

Establishing a New Normal:
Recovery Phase

After a major trauma, everything can seem different. The world suddenly seems unsafe and unpredictable—and continues to feel that way for some time to come.

This is how your people are likely to feel in the aftermath of a disaster. The common sentiment is, "We can never go back to normal around here. Things will never be the same." This is natural enough: They have been emotionally traumatized; they may be mourning; they may be frightened. As a result, it's a good idea to avoid framing the task ahead as "getting back to normal." Instead, introduce the concept of establishing "a new normal," which builds in the recognition of what has occurred while phasing back into productive work.

This is something people can understand and grasp emotionally. It can help them move forward. It removes the implication that they are being asked to act as if nothing has happened—as if Helen and Jack are still at their desks, or that irreplaceable historic building still stands, or those thousands of seals and cormorants did not suffocate in a layer of crude oil. The "new normal" sets up the expectation that there may be some changes to come in the workplace.

It's Back to Work We Go

It's best to get people back to work as soon as possible after a disaster. There is nothing normal about staying home in recovery mode. The longer people stay out, isolated and brooding over what has happened, the more abnormal things will feel. Getting people back to work, on the other hand, gives them an opportunity to process the experience together, in an organized way, which you can facilitate. It allows them to have accurate information, too, which is essential to recovery.

This is not to say that you should ask people to conduct a regular workday immediately after a catastrophic experience. Instead, the first day back at work should be a day for "slaying the dragon"—confronting what happened by, for example, returning to the building where the incident occurred. Management should be highly visible on this day. Up-to-date information should be flowing. There should be clear acknowledgment of what has occurred, and structured opportunities for asking questions and venting the very difficult reactions that people will naturally be experiencing.

Your Window of Opportunity

Crisis psychologists know that typically it is during the window of twelve to seventy-two hours following a traumatic incident that people are best able to process what they have been through.

If it is impossible for employees to go back to the workplace within seventy-two hours, you should still strive to bring everyone together. Consider having them (with their families, if appropriate to the situation) meet at an off-site location like a hotel, school or a church.

You want to avoid leaving your employees out of touch for a long period. If the incident occurred on a Friday, when employees would normally have been off until Monday, consider contacting them during the weekend with a standardized, prepared statement of up-to-date information. This could even be done on the first evening of an incident, even if people are to come back to work the next day. In severely traumatizing cases, set up a buddy system, in which employees can check in with each other until they can meet again with management.

A phone tree system in which managers and supervisors call all their direct reports is one way to accomplish this outgoing communication, and obtain an assessment of people's states of mind at the same time. In addition to delivering prepared information, questions could be asked about how each person was involved in the incident, and their needs, reactions and concerns. Those making the calls should be cautioned not to get into "counseling sessions." Callers should establish early in the conversations that calls must be short, since several contacts are to be made. Anyone who appears to be having significant difficulty could be identified and then contacted separately by a crisis-experienced mental health professional.

The First Day Back

As a general rule, management should be present, visible and accessible when people are arriving back at work for the first time. If bulletins have been prepared regarding the incident facts and the day's schedule, managers could be the ones to hand them out as employees arrive. You want to make the simple gestures of contact that let people know you are aware of what they are experiencing. Some companies have mounted large banners to welcome employees back. That's what TransAmerica Insurance Group did in Los Angeles following the 1994 Northridge earthquake.

The management briefing. The first thing that should occur on the first day back is a briefing for employees by senior management, at which attendance by all is mandatory.

The briefing will make employees feel cared for, listened to and understood. It is an opportunity to provide them with up-to-date information, and to discuss management's response actions following the incident. It is the place to squelch rumors and establish a consistent core message about what has occurred. It is the time to tell employees what to expect in the near future, and for them to ask questions. Its purpose is to provide information and show management's understanding of what employees have experienced.

During the management briefing, you should establish how ongoing communications about the crisis will take place: You may be planning additional briefings, or have set up an information telephone line or website, an e-mail or phone tree notification system, or other mechanism for keeping your people informed. Now is the time to explain these. People will want to know that they will be kept in the information loop as the situation unfolds.

Ways of listening. For most companies I have observed during crises, methods for *receiving* information tend to be less well organized than methods for *giving* information. Getting accurate and timely information from every part of your organization is vital to your ongoing management of a situation. Do not leave this function to chance. Set up a purposeful system for getting information. It might include an open door policy for top managers; a hot line or reporting line, guaranteeing anonymity if warranted; a suggestion box for written ideas; designated managers who will accept and deal with e-mailed comments; focus groups; feedback surveys following group stress debriefings; or other mechanisms for inbound communication. These should all be explained at the management briefing.

A Program for Recovery

You owe it to your people, and to the continued health of your organization, to institute a structured program that facilitates recovery and the establishment of the "new normal." In most cases, this should include group stress debriefings; individual assessment and counseling sessions; an intentional "phasing back" into productive work; ongoing supervisory monitoring; and a strategy for "disengagement" from the traumatic event.

Group stress debriefings. These sessions, conducted by skilled crisis mental health professionals, are designed to educate and reassure people, allow them to vent emotions and recognize their reactions as normal, and enhance cohesiveness and recovery. Whether employees sign up for times that are convenient or are assigned to meetings ahead of time, I recommend that everyone must attend a debriefing session. Experience has shown that if attendance is voluntary, many of those most in need of support will not come, out of fear or discomfort, and the goal of re-establishing cohesion will be undermined. No one is required to speak at these sessions, and they are not a form of psychotherapy or treatment. They are the field-tested standard of care following traumatic events, and can transform the shaken atmosphere of a traumatized workplace.

For two decades, CMI has archived the written feedback from every debriefing group we have conducted, for thousands of companies. Over 99 percent of the participants have given group debriefings a positive ranking. There are some mental health professionals who will claim that these groups should not be mandatory, or that they are harmful. I concede that too many ill-equipped "debriefers" conduct such sessions. But ask people who have gone through debriefings by highly skilled facilitators, and you will hear nearly unanimous praise.

CMI had independent research conducted on the effects of debriefing groups and structured follow up assistance for thousands of Bell South employees following Hurricane Andrew in 1992. The same research was replicated for the Oklahoma Water Resources Board, whose building was blown nine inches off its foundation by the 1995 Murrah Federal Building bombing. Both studies indicated a statistically significant reduction in the severity of traumatic stress symptomology, comparing people before and after CMI's intervention.

Group debriefings ideally should take place between twelve and seventy-two hours after the incident. Earlier than that, people are likely too numbed to put their personal reactions into words; after seventy-two hours, people typically begin to "seal over" emotionally. Ideally, group de-briefings would be scheduled for the first day back at work, as part of the collective process of re-entry.

Individual assessment and counseling. Some individuals will be identified—in group debriefings, by supervisors, by coworkers or by them-selves—as needing additional counseling and emotional support. You should make it clear to employees that they can ask for additional help for themselves and for affected family members. Make it safe for people to re-quest help. And arrange for this professional assistance to take place on-site, so it is easy for them to use.

At least some of the on-site crisis counselors should be skilled at the new "exposure therapies" for traumatic stress. One method involves rapid eye movement back and forth while thinking about distressing mental images of the incident. It is one of the most researched methods of psychological treatment, shown to be very effective for treating traumatized individuals. These treatments can rapidly reprogram the brain to still remember the in-cident while reducing the distressing mental images and overwhelming emotions. This can very rapidly get people back on their feet and back to work at an appropriate time, especially when provided in a context of car-ing management actions and group stress debriefings. As with any treat-ment modality, there are exceptions, and some people will need more in-depth assistance.

Phasing back into productive work. Just as it is crucial to acknowl-edge and memorialize the crisis and its impact, it is essential to bring the period of post-crisis processing toward a close, and get back to work. De-pending on the crisis and circumstances, you might phase into normal work on the third day; or, following any funerals. In other instances, it could take considerably longer; for example, it took three weeks before employees could return to work following the 1993 World Trade Center bombing.

You can use all kinds of symbolic but potent markers to pinpoint this transition. For instance, if you normally observe a business attire dress code, you might relax it for the immediate period following the incident, then resume the dress code on an announced day to symbolize a return to normal work. If there have been flower wreaths or banners up, establish a time to put them away. The point is to provide a moment when everyone, symbolically, resumes regular activities.

Supervisory monitoring. Managers and supervisors have an extra role to play in the aftermath of a disaster, as the eyes and ears of your recovery and human support efforts. Since they know your employees best, they are in the position to recognize those who are having continued difficulty and evidencing distress. Let supervisors know that they should be alert for unusual behavior, and whom to report it to. This is how you will identify any individuals who may need referrals for further treatment.

You should be aware that if a person continues to experience traumatic stress reactions for a month or more, they may meet the legally accepted diagnostic criteria for posttraumatic stress disorder (PTSD). By monitoring and treating employees who experience continuing stress reactions, you will be better able to avoid significant medical costs and lost productivity down the line.

Disengagement. The point will come when you can disengage your Crisis Management Team and response activities. There are a variety of indicators, both internal and external, that disengagement is appropriate.

- Is the crisis resolved to your satisfaction?
- Has media coverage of the event subsided?
- Have people and the organization found a "new normal" equilibrium that allows a return to normal productivity?
- Have rumors stopped or diminished dramatically?
- Has evidence of lingering outrage diminished?
- Have sales returned to pre-crisis levels?
- Has your stock price stabilized?

Part of disengaging is acknowledging what happened, and you may want to consider some ways to memorialize it in the future. But beware of "anniversary overkill." Many companies overprepare for the one-year anniversaries of a crisis event. But don't ignore the anniversary, either. These dates may indeed occasion some noticeable reaction in your work force. And having counselors available or a memorial gathering might be wise. But anticipating something more serious, companies sometimes call in multiple counselors or set up debriefing group opportunities that nobody feels the need to utilize. Consider doing something symbolic but restrained, like publishing an acknowledgment in the internal newsletter, placing a wreath in the lobby or inviting interested individuals to participate in a task force to talk over the lasting effects of the incident.

Operational Debriefing for Lessons Learned

In disaster and crisis management, there are two meanings for "debriefing." The group stress debriefings, which help people process what has happened to them, are different from operational debriefings, which are meant to draw lessons from how you managed the situation. It is important that you thoroughly debrief management's response, to identify both the strengths in your response and the areas that will need improvement for coping with future incidents. Also, provide group stress debriefings for your Crisis Management Team members. Their stress reactions have been pushed aside and will now surface.

Even after disengagement, with the new normal in place, consider a continuing program of monitoring your organization for lingering effects of the crisis. You will want to know, and develop a response, if you find that any of the following are occurring in a significant way.

- New and related issues arise
- Rumors concerning the crisis
- Chronically lowered morale
- Negatively affected relationships internally and externally
- Diminished consumer loyalty and trust
- Speculations or resurfacing coverage about the company in the media
- Discernible negative effects on company reputation and diminished goodwill in the eyes of the public
- Continuing financial implications

But the most valuable product of debriefing and monitoring the aftermath of this crisis will be the information it furnishes that you can use right now to prepare yourself for future disasters. In the next section of the book, I will lead you through the steps of creating a comprehensive preparedness plan for your organization. With it in place, you need never be blindsided again.

Quick Use Response Guide

CHAPTER 10: ESTABLISHING A NEW NORMAL: RECOVERY PHASE

- Did you get people back to work as soon as appropriately possible after the catastrophe?
- On the first day back at work:
  - ○ Was management highly visible?
  - ○ Was there clear acknowledgment of what occurred?
  - ○ Were there opportunities for employees to ask questions and discuss concerns?
  - ○ Did every appropriate person attend a briefing by senior management?
- Did you set up a system for giving and receiving ongoing information?
- Did you hold group stress debriefings, attended by all significantly impacted personnel, between twelve and seventy-two hours after the incident?
- Were individuals provided an opportunity for additional on-site counseling and emotional support?
- Did you frame the period of crisis aftermath processing, so that everyone knew when to phase back into normal work?
- Were managers and supervisors briefed on their role as observers, so they could recognize any people who needed additional support in readjusting?
  - ○ Were those individuals provided with professional help?
- Did your Crisis Management Team make a purposeful decision regarding when to disengage from crisis response?

- Did you debrief your crisis response performance for lessons learned, so that you can use what you learned in future preparedness planning?
- Was a group stress debriefing provided for the Crisis Management Team members?

PART 2

PREPAREDNESS

CHAPTER 11

The First Step to Preparedness

In effective crisis management, responsiveness and preparedness go hand-in-hand. These are the twin disciplines you must master to protect your company from danger. We've just looked at responsiveness. In Chapters Eleven through Twenty, we will focus on preparedness.

The financial importance of preparedness was underscored by a recent study, *The Impact of Catastrophes on Shareholder Value*, published by Templeton College, of Oxford University.

"Firms affected by catastrophes fall into two relatively distinct groups—recoverers and non-recoverers," the study found. And the recoverers actually tend to increase their shareholder value over time. "Although all catastrophes have an initial negative impact on value, paradoxically they offer an opportunity to management to demonstrate their talent in dealing with difficult circumstances." Among the essential differences between the recoverers and non-recoverers, the study concluded that "the issue of management's responsibility for accident or safety lapses appears to explain the shareholder value response."

As illustrated in this graph, the Templeton study found that after a catastrophe, there is a sharp initial negative impact on the value of a company's stock. However, those companies whose management responded well to the crisis experienced recovery, while those companies whose management did not respond effectively experienced further decline.

By being prepared and knowing how you would respond if a catastrophe hit your company today, you can lessen the financial, human and reputational aftereffects of the incident. Even if you were blindsided at this very minute, and hadn't seen a disaster that was coming your way, a plan would be in place to clearly assist your organization and employees in a produc-

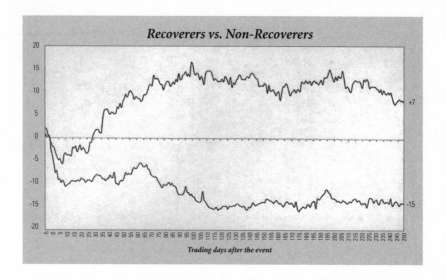

tive and meaningful way. Preparing yourself for the crises you can reason-ably anticipate will even help you respond to incidents that are totally un-expected. There is a carryover effect that will help you, no matter what occurs.

The Role of a Responsible Manager

To manage with vision, you know you must balance efforts toward growing your company with an understanding of addressing the risks it may face.

Take, for example, one vice president we worked with who had the fore-sight to initiate a corporate wide "safeness program." This senior level manager, who worked for national retailer Target Corporation, was keenly aware of the need for unparalleled safety for employees and customers.

Target instituted a comprehensive campaign for training and security, making sure that both managers and employees were acutely aware of how to respond to issues of safety. After implementation, they monitored the program to guarantee that it was effective and working well. Next, they set up a system to gauge any foreseeable threats to the organization. One per-son initiated that entire program, with the support of the senior manage-ment team.

As a manager you might have responsibility for a small work unit, or perhaps for thousands of employees. No matter the scale, you have an enormous responsibility. It begins with simple precautions and information to reduce the inherent hazards or potential dangers of your operations. Anticipation is paramount.

How Prepared Are You?

Perhaps your company has developed a crisis plan or had a few training sessions and put a training manual on every shelf. These efforts are laudable, but it is very easy to gain a false sense of security, especially if you don't allow yourself to visualize in detail the aftermath of any foreseeable incidents.

For example, an Employee Assistance Program (EAP) is a common way to address personal problems of employees and their families. Often, human resource professionals rely on EAP counseling as a sole remedy for a traumatized workforce. But you also owe it to your employees to have trained media spokespersons within your organization, and an outside public relations firm to assist with external communications. You can quickly lose control of your message and tarnish a good reputation if management doesn't protect employees from encroaching reporters and instruct them not to talk to the media.

Risk managers and their insurance brokers analyze your company's needs on a regular basis. Your company insures against foreseeable losses with carefully analyzed policy limits for various types of coverage. Shouldn't your management prepare their response for catastrophic incidents with the same care and money?

You and your management team can work effectively and look very good when you're in the crisis spotlight. The key is developing a preparedness strategy.

Don't Forget the Human Side

When an emergency occurs, the visible seems to demand our attention. We rush in to get the wounded evacuated, put out the fires, address security issues and take control of the TV crews that are suddenly turning up. And it's true that all those tasks are urgent.

But in the chaos, too many crisis managers neglect those people left behind. Since they're not bleeding, they seem not to have been significantly affected.

Maybe this is because the more visible needs seem more urgent. People's invisible, internal reactions may seem too nebulous for managers to get their arms around. What's more, there is a lingering prejudice toward psychological matters that's hard to shake.

It's also true that most people have an inherent distaste for dealing with human mortality. Our minds recoil from images of blood-splattered cubicles or killer storms that can blow people through the air. This makes us reluctant to think about people who have been victimized, especially where there are no physical symptoms.

Past approaches to crisis preparedness have tended to only skim the surface of humanitarian response. But after the bombing at the Murrah Federal Building in Oklahoma City and the September 11, 2001, attacks we all learned that catastrophes can have huge, traumatic effects on people who are not physically injured at all—or even at the scene.

Don't Take False Cover

Perhaps managers think that when it comes to the human impact of a disaster, medical benefits, workers compensation and Employee Assistance Programs will cover their crisis needs adequately. Let's look at why this is not true.

Medical benefits are commonly either underutilized or abused by employees following traumatic incidents. A symptom of traumatic stress is to avoid anything that reminds the affected individual of the incident. People try to block out the experience. Thus, some become immobilized and deny their physical and emotional symptoms. Others will overuse drugs and medical services in an attempt to cope. Both of these maladaptive solutions can cause costly long-term problems for employers and employees alike.

Workers compensation is a remedy mostly used by employees who are physically injured. In most states, uninjured employees affected by traumatic incidents in the workplace do not qualify. And some workers prefer to remain on the job without seeking benefits, perhaps out of embarrassment at admitting to psychological problems, or intimidation of the workers compensation system.

In many states, psychological injuries are not considered compensable under workers compensation law; medical treatment is covered for physical injuries only. In other states, an employee must first be physically injured before psychological injury treatment will be considered.

In only a handful of states has workers compensation coverage been available for psychological injuries for those not physically injured. Reasons offered include the cost, and the difficulty of defining successful treatment for non-physical injuries. The pendulum is swinging toward parity in mental and physical health treatment in both workers compensation and medical insurance coverage. But the inequality remains.

Employee assistance programs, meanwhile, are often not oriented or prepared to provide help in a context of crisis, beyond group debriefings and individual counseling.

Tangible and Intangible Aspects of Crisis

Among the myriad aspects of human-side response are:

- Facilitating emergency assistance to the injured
- Providing emotional first aid to affected people
- Notifying families of casualties
- Accounting for people, and arranging security to those who were on the scene
- Communicating with employees before they are sent home
- Implementing a family representative program to deal with relatives
- Visiting hospitals and homes of those injured or killed
- Assuring ongoing communications with affected constituencies
- Addressing the needs of employees on their first day back
- Orchestrating skilled professional crisis intervention services
- Determining appropriate benefits to employees during recovery
- Directing managers and supervisors in addressing the needs of traumatized employees
- Identifying "at risk" employees for follow-up assistance
- Developing an employee recovery task force
- Orchestrating appropriate memorials
- Balancing the post-incident need for caring with productivity

You can see from this partial listing that the human side of a crisis is complex, and that managing it effectively demands planning and a commitment of effort.

Your Organization Is a Human System

Just like parents in a family, management is a member of the corporate "family system," and should be an active participant in addressing the human, emotional needs of all the system's participants. Employees, customers, the media, attorneys, government regulators, the investment community and boards of directors look to management to take responsible actions following traumatic catastrophes. Management needs to be prepared to address both the content of the crisis *and* the people-side, regardless of who was physically injured.

Good vs. Poor Crisis Response

A manager's reputation—and a company's image in the marketplace—can be irreversibly altered by the handling of a workplace catastrophe.

GOOD RESPONSE

Let's consider components that indicate the aftermath of the catastrophe is being well managed:

- Immediate and decisive actions address the urgent content of the crisis, and regain control of the situation.
- The problems at hand and the potential for escalation are promptly identified.
- Responsibility is taken for solving the problems without assigning blame.
- Root causes are identified and investigated.
- An effective crisis communications plan reaches all constituents.
- Compassion and caring are demonstrated in words and actions.

- Management is accessible to affected individuals and groups, including families of casualties, injured and uninjured employees and the media.
- Ongoing steps are taken to make indicated short- and long-term changes.
- Duration of the crisis is minimized.
- There is little or no evidence of lingering outrage, damaged reputation, business disruption, negative financial impact or harm to individuals.
- Sales, stock prices and other financial indicators stabilize.

POOR RESPONSE

Indicators that a crisis has not been handled well include:

- Management responds slowly or without coordination in the immediate aftermath.
- Immediate and emerging problems, including escalation potential, are not identified.
- Actions address only surface symptoms and consequences, rather than critical components of the crisis.
- Management is reluctant to assume responsibility for cause (if appropriate) and response.
- Assessment of ongoing response needs is ineffective or slow.
- Communications to and from the Crisis Management Team are ineffective, or fail to address the needs of everyone affected.
- Management response is inadequately communicated, unknown or misunderstood.
- Caring and compassion are not communicated.
- Managers and owners are invisible and inaccessible.
- The crisis is prolonged by inaction or missteps.
- Crisis-related costs escalate over time.
- Observers express outrage and blame toward the organization.

The Process of Preparedness

Effective preparedness is based on a series of tasks that you diligently follow and practice.

I have organized these tasks into a clear, logical Six-Step Preparedness Process, which I will explain below. These will be applicable to all the crises we deal with in this book—and any other challenging scenario you might find yourself confronting.

Psychologist Albert Ellis suggested that there are irrational and self-defeating beliefs and behaviors that are common to most people. In his extensive work on the topic of human thinking and behavior, one common irrational belief he identified is that it is *easier to avoid life's problems than to face them.* Some people in your company may find it easier to avoid preparing for crises, just as some find it easier to keep smoking than to quit. With characteristic bluntness, Ellis referred to this phenomenon as "stupid behavior by non-stupid people."

The problem is not lack of intelligence, but rather that common beliefs and emotional discomforts get in the way of rational behavior. In the case of crisis preparedness, we just don't want to think about ourselves as being vulnerable. Mistaken beliefs that may keep us from implementing the Six-Step Preparedness Process include: "It won't happen here," "I have other more important things to do," and "I'll handle it when it happens."

Enlightened people are those who carefully analyze their risks and prepare. An enlightened manager does the same for his or her company. If you do, you will experience the calm assurance that comes from knowing that and your team are prepared for critical situations.

We can compare preparedness to an ongoing effort like regular exercising. You don't just say you're going to try it a few times and expect beneficial results. Optimally, it's ongoing. Doing a little bit of exercise is better than not doing any at all, but we all know that regularity is the key to staying in shape and enjoying the rewards of improved health. It's a simple equation: The more consistently you perform an appropriate exercise program, the better off you'll be. You might even save your own life.

The same is true of crisis preparedness. When it comes to your company and employees, we're talking about a regimen of preparedness exercises that just might save lives, jobs and the vitality of your organization or work unit.

There is one other piece to the equation of getting started in the preparedness process in earnest. Even though people understand what is best, they still have something that keeps them from following through. The process that holds them back is called "cognitive-emotive dissonance." This is a big term for a simple process. Mainly, it means that sometimes we must follow through even though we don't feel like it.

Think of the analogy of driving your car on the opposite side of the road. If you grew up in America, for example, your thinking (cognition) and your feelings (emotion) both tell you to drive on the righthand side of the road. But, if you were to travel to England and drive a vehicle, you would quickly experience the process of cognitive-emotive dissonance. Your rational thinking would say, "drive on the left" because you are aware that you're driving in England where they drive on the left. But, your gut level feeling would tell you to drive on the righthand side of the road, which you have been doing all your life. Even though, driving on the right-hand side of the road in England is obviously a behavior that could quickly get you and others killed, your ingrained feelings tell you to keep doing what you've always been doing—drive on the right.

The process of overcoming well-ingrained habits that are unproductive or harmful is to do what your rational thinking tells you is best, rather than what "feels comfortable in the moment." I go through this process every morning when the alarm goes off in the early hours of the morning. My gut level feeling says, "Stay in bed and get a little more sleep." But, my rational thinking tells me that I will feel much better if I get up and maintain a regular exercise routine. Here is the decision point of cognitive-emotive dissonance. Do I stay in bed, which feels better in the moment? Or, do I do what I know in my rational thinking is best, namely, get out of bed and exercise, which helps me feel better later on?

The same process applies to overeating, stopping smoking and other self-defeating habits that need changing. All it takes is to do what your rational thinking says is the correct and beneficial thing to do, even though you may not feel comfortable doing it at the time. This concept also applies to crisis preparedness. Even though it may not feel like the best thing to do right now, you will praise the day you prepared when crisis time hits. Once you decide to get yourself crisis prepared, the next step is to follow a methodical process, outlined below in my six-step process.

The Six-Step Preparedness Process

This preparedness process applies across the board, to any crisis situation. I call this field-tested system the "A, E, I, O, U and Sometimes Y" approach to preparedness.

Step 1: Analyze
Step 2: Evaluate
Step 3: Identify
Step 4: Organize
Step 5: Utilize
Step 6: Scrutinize Yourselves

This process gives you a way to sequentially address the risks inherent to your organization. It also allows you flexibility to address these hazards in a manner that fits your culture, budgetary constraints and availability of time. Here's how it works.

Analyze. First, analyze the risks that are unique to your organization and industry. Chapter Thirteen will take you through this process.

Evaluate. Next, you assess the procedures, policies and other controls that are already in place to address the identified risks. Evaluate how you can enhance these existing controls with a minimum investment of new resources. Chapter Fourteen will show you how.

Identify. You then pinpoint the new policies, procedures and other management controls that will fill in any gaps in your existing strategy. This way, you make sure you have considered a comprehensive defense for each of your identified risks. We'll discuss this in Chapter Fifteen.

Organize. Here you begin the planning process. You establish your priorities. You set timelines. You break your goals down into doable tasks. Chapter Sixteen will walk you through.

Utilize. Chapter Seventeen looks at the process of executing your plan according to your corporate culture, budgetary constraints and time frame.

Scrutinize yourselves. Only ongoing monitoring will ensure that your procedures are, in fact, working. Regularly scheduled reviews are an essential part of the preparedness process. This is the subject of Chapter eighteen.

Applying the Six Steps

Now let's take a look at a hypothetical example of how you can apply the Six-Step Preparedness Process to the possibility of workplace violence within your organization.

Step 1: Analyze. In this case, you will want to analyze the possible motives for workplace violence. Do you have a polarized workforce, perhaps as the result of union-management conflicts, where tensions could lead to violence? Do you have cash registers where robbery could be a motive for violence? Do you have a large number of women in the workplace whose presence might increase the possibility of domestic violence creeping into your facilities, when out-of-control husbands show up?

Step 2: Evaluate. Next, you will examine the existing controls you have in place that address identified motives for violence. To deal with union/management conflicts, you may have, among other things, an arbitration process for disputes. For robberies, you might have bright lighting, surveillance cameras and strict procedures for depositing money. For domestic violence, you may have an Employee Assistance Program (EAP) where employees can receive confidential counseling regarding domestic concerns.

Then you will evaluate ways to enhance these existing programs. Possibly, in addition to arbitration, a more wide-ranging program of Alternative Dispute Resolution could be established. For robberies, signs could be publicly displayed announcing that cameras are in use. And for domestic violence in the workplace, a review of the internal policies and procedures for how your EAP handles potentially violent situations could be implemented.

Step 3: Identify. Here you will begin to recognize weaknesses in your existing preparedness efforts. The objective will be to identify new defensive policies, procedures and controls to put into place. Setting up a Threat Notification System and a zero-tolerance policy that is publicized throughout the workplace might minimize employee/supervisor violence. For robberies, a safe with timed access could prohibit robberies and minimize financial losses. Implementing awareness and response training throughout your organization might curtail domestic violence in the workplace.

Step 4: Organize. This is the planning process where you prioritize and organize your prevention and post-incident responses for each identified risk. You may need to establish an implementation schedule over time if all your identified enhancements and new controls cannot be put into operation immediately.

Step 5: Utilize. Implementation of your plan is the next step. Here, you will utilize the methods that were identified and prioritized to address your identified risks.

Step 6: Scrutinize Yourselves. The last step is to establish a management information system that allows you to track the success of your programs on an ongoing basis. Annual or periodic reporting about the effectiveness and success of your prevention and post-incident programs would be reported to senior management to determine if changes are needed.

Putting the Six Steps into Action

To demonstrate how this process can work for any risk, here's another example and how the six basic steps apply. Take, for example, air travel. Before the events of September 11, 2001, you may not have thought at length about whether an executive of your company might be hijacked, or killed, while flying on business. If your senior level management travels by air, a careful application of the six-step process would prepare you ahead of time should an air tragedy occur involving your people. Consider how a crisis preparedness plan would affect this situation proactively.

Step 1: Analyze. You identify the foreseeable risk that executives in your organization could be killed in an air crash, especially given your new awareness of terrorism.

Step 2: Evaulate. You determine that you already have a policy that senior managers are not to fly together on the same flights. However, this policy has sometimes been breached in the past. An enhancement of it would involve a recommitment by the CEO and Board of Directors that no two senior-level executives will fly on the same flight together.

Step 3: Identify. In this process of thinking about what would happen if a senior executive were to be killed in a plane crash, you realize the need for a formalized succession plan.

Step 4: Organize. The Board of Directors and CEO might meet to develop a succession plan by identifying internal candidates who could be groomed to take over for senior managers who were killed or disabled. Additionally, a headhunter could be retained to keep a listing of qualified candidates who would be appropriate in senior management ranks of your organization.

Step 5: Utilize. The organization might implement a mentoring process to groom the identified candidates for senior-level assignments. Hiring of upper-level managers might take into consideration the ability of candidates to replace selected senior executive team members.

Step 6: Scrutinize Yourselves. Lastly, the Board of Directors would schedule six-month and annual reviews of the executive travel practices and succession plan to assure they protect the needs of the organization in case senior managers were victims of air crashes or terrorism.

Quick Use Preparedness Guide

CHAPTER 11: THE FIRST STEP TO PREPAREDNESS

- The responsible manager:
  - ○ Balances attention to company growth with attention to foreseeable risks
  - ○ Develops a thorough and comprehensive preparedness strategy
  - ○ Confronts, rather than avoids, uncomfortable issues
  - ○ Never overlooks the human factor
- The Six-Step Preparedness Plan employs the "A, E, I, O, U and Sometimes Y" method:
  - ○ Analyze
    - ■ What are your foreseeable risks?
  - ○ Evaluate
    - ■ What procedures, policies and controls are in place to address your risks?
    - ■ What needs to be strengthened?
  - ○ Identify

- Identify new controls to supplement existing policies and procedures.
○ Organize
  - Organize and plan out your crisis response strategies.
○ Utilize
  - Execute and utilize your plan according to an implementation schedule that fits your budget, time and corporate culture.
○ Scrutinize Yourselves
  - Initiate an ongoing process to monitor your processes, procedures and controls for effectiveness.

CHAPTER 12

Setting Up a Crisis Planning Committee

The word "committee" tends to induce a groan. But corralling the right group of people to execute the Six-Step Preparedness Process we discussed in the previous chapter is imperative to your success. Before you can take the first step, you must create a Crisis Planning Committee, or CPC.

Selecting a CPC is a lot like building your dream house. That's a big challenge, and one you can't possibly take on alone. The ultimate decisions may be up to you, but you need to rely on your architect, contractor, landscape architect and interior designer for the best advice.

In this chapter, we'll discuss two things:

- Why you need a Crisis Planning Committee
- How to set one up

Why You Need a Crisis Planning Committee

It may be tempting to go it alone, but that would be a mistake. There are three compelling reasons why every company should have a formal Crisis Planning Committee:

- Access to multidisciplinary perspectives
- Team decision-making
- Legal defensibility

Let's take a look at the power in numbers.

Strength in Variety: Multidisciplinary Perspectives

When you build your CPC, you will want to draw from the many disciplines or departments in your company, as well as from resources outside your company. The more perspectives you have, and the more varied the expertise, the more comprehensive your outlook will be.

For example, if your building is exposed to a toxic substance, your human resources department may be concerned about what kind of medical or psychological trauma assistance your employees will require. Your facility management, meanwhile, will need to understand how the exposure occurred, and take steps to bring the building back up to healthy, habitable standards again. Your legal staff will want to ensure that liability is limited. And so on.

Nobody knows all the answers, but input from multiple sources will raise considerations you would otherwise overlook. Diverse people forge a thorough solution.

Why Team Decision-Making Works

Decision by committee—it's almost a punch line, to a joke about something that doesn't work very well. But in crisis planning, team decisions are best. Good crisis planning balances the perspectives of many in a task-oriented mode. You want a lean, crisp team that is empowered and has a sense of urgency. Together, they can tackle the complex risks that you will identify—better than even the most brilliant manager ever could.

Suppose you try to do all of this work yourself, and then a disaster strikes. Inevitably, questions will arise about how well you were prepared. Your work may be criticized.

If you did that work alone, full responsibility for any failure will fall on you. But if you worked with a Crisis Preparedness Committee, you will be able to honestly say: "We brought together the best people we could find. They represented all the important units of our organization, and a wide range of expertise. Every decision we made was the result of an open group process. We did our best."

A Daunting Task Demands a Strong Group Effort

I once got a call from a risk manager at a national fast-food chain. He was the guy assigned to put together a crisis management plan. Alone. This manager had a lot on his plate and kept procrastinating. He had no information, no management support, no budget and no expertise outside his discipline of risk management.

Clearly, he felt overwhelmed. Although well meaning, he keep going off on tangents—surfing the Web, reading articles and trying to figure out what to do and how to proceed. He didn't know enough about business operations, or the human side of crisis, or public relations practice. He knew solely about risk and insurance management. He was in way over his head, and poised to fail.

We met briefly. But his leaders had given him no resources and only a vague mandate, so he lost momentum. Five years later, he still didn't have his crisis management plan in place. It kept falling to the bottom of his to-do list. The company has already experienced one serious incident. If a similar incident occurs again—a high probability in their industry—tough questions will arise regarding their lack of prevention. Would you like to be in his position?

Conversely, CMI assisted a large, multinational company, with more than 300,000 employees, in their crisis planning process. This firm brought in a senior level group of managers from across the country and around the globe to serve on their CPC.

The scope of the project was daunting. The company had international ground and air operations, distribution centers, facilities where the public was admitted, numerous office buildings and multiple locations, each with its own inherent risks.

There was little standardization in tracking or reporting. The various regions were not aware of the critical incidents that occurred in their own areas, much less in the others.

Still, they were committed to being crisis prepared. They called us in at the start to set up a system to guide them to a swift, successful completion. With diligence and collective effort, they had an action plan and a response system in place six weeks later. They followed the steps outlined below, and in subsequent chapters, to get there.

How to Set Up a Crisis Planning Committee

Just as important as deciding to have a committee is how you set it up. A number of considerations must be met to ensure the group's ultimate success:

- Determine the scope.
- Identify champions.
- Select the members.
- Set an agenda.
- Establish a budget.
- Make a schedule.
- Conduct the meetings.

Now, let's examine each step in greater depth.

Determine the Scope

Before you choose your CPC, you must step back and take a large-scale view of your company. Ask yourself these questions to come up with the scope of the project you are undertaking.

- What are your objectives and expected deliverables?
- Is this a local, regional, national or international project?
- Will your plan be rolled out company-wide or piloted in selected areas?
- Do you have an existing plan that needs improving, or are you starting from scratch?
- What areas of foreseeable risks and concerns do you want to address?
- How high a priority is this project? How much support does it have from senior management?
- How much authority will the CPC have to do its job?

Identify Champions

Champions are leaders, a committee's driving force. There are typically two champions in company crisis planning: a senior-level champion, and a logistical champion.

The senior-level champion is the visionary. He or she ensures that the right financial and human tools are in place to make the CPC a success, and provides top management support. He or she will delegate to the logistical champion.

The logistical champion will actually lead the CPC through its process. A good logistical champion is someone who has the passion and authority to make sure that the CPC's objectives and goals are met. This person must understand the scope of the project and agree with the mission. The job requires deep commitment to the process, and the ability to invest the time to bring it to fruition. Ideally, this person will have deep and wide company contacts, and will be respected by people at all levels in the organization. He or she must have sufficient authority to make things happen. Without the right person in this role, it will be difficult for the CPC to succeed.

Select the CPC Members

Getting the right mix of people is critical. You want a blend of disciplines, as we discussed, and a blend of personalities as well. It's important to include both task-oriented and people-oriented members. A balance of creative and analytical types is also good.

Depending on your corporate culture, you may either appoint members or invite people to participate. No matter which you choose, it would be wise to bring in an attorney (whether on staff or outside counsel) to formalize the assignment.

Why You Need an Attorney

Your committee is going to do its genuine best to prepare your company for disaster. But after the dust of a calamity has cleared, your preparedness process is likely to be second-guessed anyway. In the worst case, your company may be sued for negligence and liability.

Having an attorney involved in your Crisis Preparedness Committee offers a type of insurance through attorney-client privilege. It won't prevent your being sued, but it will leave you better prepared to defend yourselves in court.

The attorney's job on the CPC is to make sure that the committee does not generate any documentary material that could later be used against you in court. The attorney should supervise the consolidation and approval of any notes produced in the course of the committee's work. By the conclusion of your preparedness process, you want to end up with a single version of what you have done—one that a lawyer has approved. Then you should shred everything else as a matter of policy. This approved version becomes the documentation of your committee's work. The attorney, under privilege, should house it. Some organizations go as far as keeping everything verbal until this single report is prepared.

What you want to avoid is producing a record that could show that your committee knew of weaknesses or gaps in your crisis defense strategy, and failed to address them.

Attorney-client privilege isn't airtight. But it increases your protection—in effect, protecting you from yourselves.

The Composition of Your Committee

Besides having a mix of personality types on the CPC, you will want to have a mix of disciplines represented. Here are some people to consider having on the CPC:

- Attorney (as just discussed)
- Continuity or contingency planner
- Information technology manager
- Human resources manager
- Government compliance administrator
- Risk and insurance manager
- Financial manager
- Medical director
- Law enforcement officer

- Security manager
- Public relations director
- Crisis management consultant

How big should your CPC be? I can't give you a definitive answer. In the 300,000-employee company I mentioned above, fifty people were enough to get the job done, although they broke into smaller sub-committees to handle specific tasks. As a general rule, the smallest CPC contains five people. Twelve is a good maximum number, for efficiency. Anything larger requires breaking into sub-committees.

But you must base the size of your CPC on such variables as corporate culture, company size, the scope of the job, budget and other factors. The key is to balance the effectiveness a multidisciplinary committee can bring with the efficiency of the smallest possible team.

Select a Consultant

A consultant often serves as a facilitator at CPC meetings. A consultant is also an invaluable resource to the champion by bringing expertise and knowledge of other companies to the table. So how do you select a good consultant? This person or firm should be prominent in the field of crisis preparedness, and it's even better if they have experience in your industry.

A good consultant will work to identify both weaknesses and positive aspects of your crisis management plan. No one consultant has all the expertise you will need, but the good firms fill the gap with affiliations to other consultants. Crisis preparedness consultants tend to charge either project or retainer fees.

Set an Agenda

Determine what topics need to be discussed at each meeting and what "homework" needs to be done before and after each meeting. The agenda should follow the Six-Step Preparedness Process.

For example, in the first CPC meeting, you may want to analyze the vulnerabilities inherent to your organization and examine the existing procedures that correspond to these risks. To facilitate that first meeting, you might ask members to arrive armed with data about the risks each knows about.

Establish a Budget

To run an effective CPC, you will need money. Working with senior management, you will need to outline the costs you expect to incur for such items as hotel accommodations, transportation, meals, materials, reports, consultants and other needs. Be sure to budget about 10 to 20 percent more than you think you'll need so you aren't stalled midway by lack of funds.

A preliminary budget could pay for expenses to run the Crisis Planning Committee. You could make a fuller request later, when you have a better idea of your full crisis preparedness needs.

Make a Schedule

Before you can decide how often to meet, how long each meeting should last and the location of each meeting, you will need to consider a number of items:

- What are your objectives and deliverables?
- How quickly must the plan be completed?
- What is the time availability of members?
- What will it cost to bring the committee together?
- How much research must be accomplished between meetings?
- Do you want a minimum number of meetings, or does your culture value the brainstorming that comes from more frequent gatherings?

Optimally, this should be discussed during the first planning meeting. We have observed success in many companies that use reverse sequence planning to create a schedule and a timeline for the CPC. This simply involves starting with the desired outcome and working backward to see what it will take to accomplish the goal.

Once the preceding steps are in place, you are ready to bring the CPC together. The rest of this book will describe the topics that need be covered to put a successful crisis management plan into place.

Conduct the Meetings

Once your CPC members are in place, you can determine how, when and where to meet. The CPC can meet in person, via conference call or via videoconferencing. My recommendation is that you make a commitment to meet face-to-face, at least periodically. You may have one committee or several smaller sub-committees. You may meet on-site or off-site.

What to Avoid as a CPC

Committees can get sidetracked into non-productive behaviors. The key is to recognize them, eliminate them and move on in a positive manner. Some errors include:

- Failing to use an attorney to compile committee information and meeting notes, failing to ensure that documentation is written in a legally defensible manner, and failing to protect documentation, to the fullest extent possible, under attorney-client privilege
- Lack of confidentiality by CPC members regarding information that spells out your company's weaknesses
- Failing to address uncomfortable issues, or to give credence to the full range of possible risks. Avoiding questions such as, "If we were terrorists, how would we take this company to its knees?
- Engaging in denial: "It can't happen here."
- Alarmism—a Chicken Little mentality that causes members to feel overwhelmed and cry that the sky is falling on their heads
- Failing to prioritize the process enough to complete the project
- Identifying risks without taking any actions to prepare for them
- Failing to monitor your preparedness plan for effectiveness, and to update it for new risks that may emerge

Quick Use Preparedness Guide

CHAPTER 12: SETTING UP A
CRISIS PLANNING COMMITTEE

- Have you addressed the rationale for having a CPC?
  - Multidisciplinary approach
  - Team decision-making
  - Defensibility
- Setting up a CPC includes:
  - Determining the scope
  - Identifying a champion
  - Selecting members
  - Setting an agenda
  - Establishing a budget
  - Making a schedule
  - Conducting meetings
- Have you considered utilizing an attorney for attorney-client privilege?
- Have you considered utilizing a consultant to facilitate the process and lend expertise?
- What to avoid:
  - Failing to use an attorney
  - Lack of confidentiality
  - Failing to address uncomfortable issues
  - Engaging in denial
  - Alarmism
  - Failing to make the process a priority
  - Identifying risks without taking any actions
  - Failing to monitor your preparedness plan

CHAPTER 13

Analyzing Your Vulnerabilities

In a moment, the world you live in can change forever. The situations and locations can vary greatly, but tragic and unexpected traumatic events occur with alarmingly frequency.

In 1993, the World Trade Center had been bombed. The horrific attack eight years later in 2001, which blindsided the world, reminded us that lightning, indeed, can strike the same place twice. The searing images we saw repeatedly on news reports made terror real. They drove home for all of us how a crisis can shatter our workplaces—and our world—in just a split second.

We are all vulnerable to some degree, in both our personal and professional lives, regardless of where we live or what we do. This challenges each company to courageously examine its risks, and move to protect itself, its employees and its assets with a solid plan of defense.

No one has a crystal ball, or can predict where the next disaster will occur. But if we can begin to look at our organizations with a critical eye, we can discover where a door or window may be open, unwittingly inviting crisis in.

In the previous chapter, we covered how to build a multidisciplinary Crisis Planning Committee to analyze your foreseeable risks. In this chapter, I will give you the tools you need to empower that committee, so it can ready your company for possible disaster.

When you understand and prepare for the potential risks that might happen, you stack the cards in your favor, even for the unforeseeable. To assist you, in this chapter I will address the "A" of the "A, E, I, O, U and Sometimes Y" Six-Step Preparedness Process. You will learn to analyze:

- How societal change has generated risks
- The ripple effect of vulnerability
- The foreseeable risks for your company
- The role of severity and probability in prioritizing your risks
- How to protect your three core assets
- A checklist of related corporate concerns

How Societal Change Has Generated Risks

The modern workplace bears almost no resemblance to the one in which our grandparents and parents labored. We are a transient society now, less connected to our families and employers. Most of us can expect to be employed by seven different companies during our careers, and to change industries as well. Many of us will be downsized—often more than once—during our careers.

The overwhelming majority of high-fatality disasters in all history have happened in the past twenty years. This is easy to understand when you consider, for example, how our formerly agrarian landscape has changed: taller buildings with thousands of people working in them, increased foreign travel, threats of bioterrorism, chemical warfare, more and faster everything. Markets are global, and the pressure to achieve is pervasive. In addition, the workplace is less homogenous than it once was. Societal and workplace diversity has made us more dynamic and well-rounded and provided wonderful opportunities for learning and growth. But it also spawns misunderstandings, some of which explode into accidents or violence. Research has shown that workplace violence goes up during and immediately after layoffs. Sabotage and accidents also increase.

All of these societal changes create risks and set the stage for potential disasters.

The Ripple Effect of Vulnerability

Years of observing crisis situations have driven home to me the ripple effect of vulnerability. One breach can open up multiple weaknesses. The ripple effect helps to explain why disasters often spiral out of control.

Media spin, demanding customers, government regulators, resistant insurance companies, community outrage or lost production can fan the flames of a small crisis, as the wind feeds a brushfire. And the crisis can touch off new blazes in places you hadn't expected.

This effect was easy to see during the days that followed September 11, 2001. First, airports and airlines were seen as unacceptably vulnerable. Airports closed temporarily, and many workers lost their jobs. The effect rippled out to restaurants, parking lots, rental car counters and hotels, which in turn necessitated laying workers off. Many businesses in travel and other industries lost business; some went bankrupt. Overall, an estimated 1.6 million workers lost their jobs as a result of the terrorist attacks.

Employees, shareholders, customers and the press—none of these groups is as forgiving as we'd like them to be during a crisis. If we as managers can't deliver on our promises, or are seen as irresponsible, we place our companies in grave danger. If your company doesn't have an effective contingency plan in place, your livelihood could be at stake.

Analyzing Foreseeable Risks

What events would severely disrupt your operations? What are you unprepared for?

Analyzing foreseeable risks involves uncovering probable incidents that could affect your organization, so that you can minimize your risk of being blindsided.

Don't wait for a plaintiff attorney, government regulator, investigative reporter or jury to decide what risks you should have foreseen—after a disaster has occurred.

If they show that you have inadequately assessed and prepared for foreseeable risks, your company could be found guilty of negligence or blame in the court of public opinion—or a courtroom.

Almost no one blamed the management of the Murrah Federal Building in Oklahoma City following the bombing there in 1996. Why not? It was considered unforeseeable that someone would act against the residents of that city in response to events that had occurred in Waco, Texas. The same is true of the companies that were housed in the World Trade Center. However, the media and plaintiff attorneys will still try to assign blame. This is how they sell advertising and earn contingency fees.

Thinking About Likely Scenarios

It is impossible to prepare for every catastrophe your company might experience. You must develop a hierarchy of likely scenarios.

Here are some sample factors to consider. Your company might:

- Deal with dangerous equipment
- Work in a tall building for which evacuation is complex
- Have unprotected parking lots at every facility
- Give frequent tours of your premises to outside visitors
- Have unsecured points of ingress and egress
- Experience threats and demonstrations at shareholder meetings
- Send employees to international destinations known for kidnappings, extortions or political uprisings
- Use tanker trucks to carry hazardous or explosive materials
- Work in an aging building that is not up to code
- Have an internally hostile workforce
- Operate where there are floods, hurricanes, volcanoes or tornadoes

What's Likely to Happen?
Analyzing Crisis Probability

At CMI, we typically ask corporate managers, "What is the likelihood that each incident we consider would happen to you within the next decade?" You may choose a different time frame of course; what's important is to quantify your risks. In general, the more specific you can be about the probability of various events, the more accurate your predictions will become. Specificity is also important when it comes to ranking the events.

Remember to clearly define what you mean by each vulnerability or risk. A fire can be serious or minor. A product defect can result in an easy fix or a catastrophe.

Choosing the consequence is also important. For example, you may classify as serious a fire that disrupts operations for more than one day, results in specified damages to facilities and equipment, or causes critical injuries.

There are a variety of ways to analyze your company's risks—but all of them depend on good information.

You need to know what has already happened in the past to your company and to others like it. You need to know about conditions in all the places where you operate. And you need to know about the political, commercial and social tensions in the world at large. Here is a checklist to get you started:

- **Query your staff.** It's easy to overlook one's resources. Ask selected managers, supervisors and employees about the vulnerable spots they've noticed. In addition to gleaning information, this approach can uncover employees with a natural awareness of risks. Later, you might enlist some of these people to help monitor your preparedness efforts.

- **Surveys.** Written surveys or questionnaires given to employees and other important constituents can help you discover information useful to analyzing foreseeable risks and crisis planning.

- **Review history.** What incidents have happened at your company already? Is there a preponderance of a certain type? Have certain types of equipment been involved? Do incidents occur more frequently on certain days or in a certain month? With certain types of personnel— say, contracted workers vs. company employees? Or on certain shifts?

- **Review near-misses.** What near-crises have you and others in your industry experienced? These are fertile but often-overlooked indicators of pending crises. The FAA reports multiple *near misses* on runways and in the air near the world's busy airports. One can conclude that the likelihood of two planes colliding at or near an airport in the next ten years is high—so it's wise to prepare for the aftermath of such a crash today if you have multiple frequent flyers.

- **Review industry mishaps.** Educate yourself on crises that have occurred to competitors and others in your industry. Has the industry suffered a certain type of crisis again and again?

- **Assess your locations.** Geography plays a major role in the type of crisis your company might encounter. If you have facilities around the globe, each location implies unique threats. Civil unrest, for example, may be more likely in South Asia than in the Caribbean.

- **Investigate local crime and labor statistics.** A good look at crime statistics can pinpoint relevant trends. If you have a plant in Los Angeles, that area's gang activity could be a significant risk factor for you.

- **Conduct online research.** Internet research services are invaluable. One powerful resource is LexisNexis, which returns full-text articles from 30,000 databases. Unlike some Internet search engines such as Google, it is not free—and subscriptions are relatively costly. However, you can buy short-term access, which could be enough.

After conducting this thorough analysis of your situation, you will be added to list the probable risks to which your organization is vulnerable.

How Bad Could It Be? Analyzing Crisis Severity

Once you've determined your probable risks, you must analyze which of them could be most damaging. Armed robberies may be probable at a bank, but if they do not involve fatalities or large sums, they should not do too much damage. On the other hand, a major fire could devastate an unprepared company, destroying irreplaceable data and possibly costing lives.

Your Crisis Planning Committee will have arrived at definitions of your vulnerabilities, as we discussed above. For each identified risk, ask yourselves this question:

If it happened, how severely would it hurt us?

Protecting Your Three Core Assets

A company must protect three core assets: its people, its finances and its reputation. Significant damage to any one of those assets can cripple a company. As a body needs its heart, brain and lungs, a company needs all three core assets to be healthy.

- **People:** includes employees and their expertise, as well as your vendors, investors and customers.
- **Finances:** includes cash, stock value, credit rating, capital equipment and other areas of vital financial strength.
- **Reputation:** the positive feelings people have for your company. This includes how trustworthy, responsive and solid your company is perceived to be.

Let's look at a few of the ways that these integrated company assets affect each other.

People. It is in this area that most companies in crisis are least prepared to cope. Often there are plans to deal with seriously or fatally injured employees. But there is also a pressing need to address all those who are emotionally wounded and outraged. When management actively demonstrates a concern for people's emotional well-being, recovery is quicker. Employees are more productive and loyal, and their morale is higher.

Finances. Some companies pay the ultimate price after a disaster: They go out of business. Such was the case with a printing company called Standard Gravure, in Louisville, Kentucky. A fire diminished the company's operational capacities. A year after the fire, employee Joseph Wesbecker, who was on a leave of absence for a stress-related illness, returned to the workplace and shot twenty-one people, killing eight. The company worked with a PR firm and Crisis Management International, and successfully battled insurers for coverage. Still, despite management's best efforts, the company folded.

Reputation. Consider the quick fall from grace experienced by the airport security company Argenbright. In 1999, a business writer at the *Detroit Free Press* described the company as having a "sterling international reputation . . . Argenbright is known as a top aviation security contractor, with savvy management and smart hiring and training practices." At that time, although millions of air travelers routinely passed through security checkpoints run by Argenbright, few even knew the company's name.

But on September 11, 2001, terrorist hijackers successfully slipped through Argenbright-run checkpoints. We all know the horrible consequences. In the cascade of criticism that followed, Argenbright's public relations response appeared nonexistent. Suddenly, this was the company everybody loved to hate—deserving or not, it became a target for the profound anger and frustration felt by the entire country. By November, a writer in the Lansing, Michigan, *State Journal* voiced an opinion that had become nearly universal: "Argenbright has quite the reputation in aviation circles—for not doing criminal background checks, for not training people properly and for not keeping an eye on employees." The company was unprepared to respond, and as a result its public reputation was shot.

The Five Questions of Blame

There is one other area of reputational damage that must be addressed before we move on to prioritizing our foreseeable risks. The severity of any crisis can escalate significantly if there is *blame toward the company*. Blame occurs when management is seen as negligent or uncaring. Five questions define whether management will receive blame after a catastrophe:

- Should management have *foreseen* the incident and have taken adequate precautions to prevent it?
- Was management *unprepared* to respond effectively to the incident after it occurred?
- Did management do anything *intentionally* that caused the incident to occur or that made it more severe?
- Was management *unjustified* in the actions it took leading up to and following the incident?
- Is there any type of *scandal* or cover-up that is related to management's involvement in this incident?

If the answer to any of the above five questions is yes, then the company is likely to take some heavy criticism.

Following catastrophes, people are looking for someone or something to blame. When people lay blame it enables them to demand a change that will hopefully keep this from ever happening again.

Man-made catastrophes such as explosions, crashes, fires, workplace violence, terrorism and large industrial accidents all carry the possibility of high levels of public blame. Even in "acts of God," like weather-related incidents, people will look to man-made causes for the damage they have suffered. Following Hurricane Andrew's devastating landfall in Miami in 1992, a rising chorus of blame emerged during the days following the storm. People were outraged that the south Florida government and the local builders had allowed physical structures to be built without "hurricane straps" on the roofs.

As a general rule, no matter what your critical incident may be, if there is blame toward management or the company, the severity of the incident will increase significantly. You need to be ready to manage outrage just as you are ready to put out physical fires. This involves more than putting the correct public relations spin on the incident. It involves management demonstrating preparedness. It means the corporation is ready to accept responsibility for the incident, if appropriate, and for responding effectively to affected people.

Plotting Probability and Severity on the Foreseeable Risk Analysis Grid

We use a simple grid to show the relative likelihood and severity of a company's foreseeable risks. The grid is a tool that allows us to compare all identified vulnerabilities to one other, so that we can prioritize efforts to prepare for them. It looks like this:

Foreseeable Risk Analysis Grid

3			
	LOW PROBABILITY *HIGH SEVERITY*	MEDIUM PROBABILITY *HIGH SEVERITY*	HIGH PROBABILITY *HIGH SEVERITY*
2			
	LOW PROBABILITY *MEDIUM SEVERITY*	MEDIUM PROBABILITY *MEDIUM SEVERITY*	HIGH PROBABILITY *MEDIUM SEVERITY*
1			
	LOW PROBABILITY *LOW SEVERITY*	MEDIUM PROBABILITY *LOW SEVERITY*	HIGH PROBABILITY *LOW SEVERITY*

⇑SEVERITY
⇒PROBABILITY   1   2   3

To fill in the grid, you first identify your risks, through the analytic process we discussed above. Next, you assess their potential severity. Then each one is placed in the appropriate box, according to both its low, medium or high probability and severity. This exercise will help ensure that you identify and prepare most for those crises with the greatest potential impact.

It's important to be specific in naming your risks, so that you can reasonably assess the impact, or severity, each one could have. For example, "workplace violence" is too broad a phrase. A fistfight may be highly probable in a factory setting, but its effect may have low severity. Conversely, a shooting by a disturbed employee may be improbable, but its consequences would be severe.

Let's look at a hypothetical list of risks, and see how to assess and plot them on the grid. Your list will probably be somewhat longer, but for now suppose you have agreed that your company faces these six risks:

- Domestic violence intruding into the workplace. Past incident: One of your female employees took her children to a shelter to escape battering by her out-of-work husband. Enraged and armed, the man threatened to shoot her at work, where he knew he would find her.
- Fire or an explosion in your factory, where volatile materials are stored under pressure.
- Hurricane: One of your plants is located on the Texas Gulf Coast, where storms often come ashore, usually with few consequences.
- Biological attack through the mail: Deranged individuals with an anti-capitalist rationale have been sending infectious agents to corporate targets within your industry.
- Kidnapping, for ransom, workers who are located in Colombia and Ecuador near your South American operations.
- Toxic leak from the chemical plant next door, which has a long history of safety problems and incompetent management.

Each member of your Crisis Planning Committee should individually consider these six identified risks, to come up with a numerical ranking for the probability and severity for each. You might make this a homework assignment, to be done between meetings using research sources like those suggested above, possibly divided by region or operating location. Or the research could be compiled prior to the initial Crisis Planning Committee meeting. This advance work provides the basis for an informed discussion of each risk by the committee.

Have each member assign each risk a simple numeric value, separately for its probability and severity: low=1, medium=2 and high=3. Then, average all the rankings together. Once you have compiled your committee members' best estimates, you can plot them on the grid.

For example, let's assume the average of the scores for the risk of a major fire or explosion was 1.5 in probability, and 2.4 in severity. You would place this risk in the top/middle box as illustrated in the grid on page 146. Let's suppose, just for example, you ranked your other five risks as follows:

- Domestic violence (physical assault with serious injuries) intruding into the workplace: probability 1.4, medium; severity 1.9, medium.
- Fire or explosion in your factory: probability 1.6, medium; severity 2.6, high.
- Hurricane: probability 2.8, high; severity 1, low.
- Biological attack through the mail: probability 1, low; severity 3, high.
- Kidnapping of executives traveling to inspect foreign operations: probability 2.6, high; severity 1.7, medium.
- Leak from the next-door chemical plant: probability 3, high; severity 2.7, high.

You would place them on the grid like this:

Foreseeable Risk Analysis Grid

LOW PROBABILITY *HIGH SEVERITY* biological attack through the mail	MEDIUM PROBABILITY *HIGH SEVERITY* fire or explosion	HIGH PROBABILITY *HIGH SEVERITY* leak from next door
LOW PROBABILITY *MEDIUM SEVERITY*	MEDIUM PROBABILITY *MEDIUM SEVERITY* domestic violence	HIGH PROBABILITY *MEDIUM SEVERITY* kidnappings abroad
LOW PROBABILITY *LOW SEVERITY*	MEDIUM PROBABILITY *LOW SEVERITY*	HIGH PROBABILITY *LOW SEVERITY* hurricane

⇑SEVERITY

⇒PROBABILITY   1   2   3

You want to prioritize your preparedness plans to deal with the most probable and most severe risks you can identify. Those are the ones that fall into the four *shaded* cells at the upper right. Of course, at your company, some boxes may contain more than one risk.

The risks that fall outside those four top-priority boxes should still get attention, but less. While you have agreed, for example, that a biological attack on your company through the mail is unlikely, you have also agreed that its severity could be high. You certainly cannot ignore it. But by using the Foreseeable Risk Analysis Grid you have been able to make a rational decision about its relative importance.

Additional Considerations in Assessing Severity

In addition to the threats to your three core assets—people, finances and reputation—your company's well-being faces a number of other risks. Some companies are engaged in inherently dangerous operations. Banks and retail operations are often the targets of robbery. Oil and chemical companies must plan for explosions and leaks. Manufacturing facilities face industrial accidents. Transportation providers suffer accidents. Hospitals see emergency room violence. Companies that do business in politically unstable countries can subject people to kidnapping or terrorist incidents.

When you are using the Foreseeable Risk Analysis Grid to prioritize your company's actual vulnerabilities, you will want to consider all the factors that could affect severity. These include:

- **Legal concerns:** Extreme liability is more likely in companies that are unprepared. In 1993, an insurance company that was the scene of a tragic triple murder by a disgruntled former employee called me to Tampa. It later emerged that the killer's previous managers, at Allstate Insurance Company, had encouraged him to leave his job at that company. Paul Calden had a contentious history. He spoke of aliens controlling his mind, threatened coworkers and routinely carried a gun in his briefcase. Allstate thought it was ridding itself of the troublesome Calden when it gave him a severance package. It also gave him a letter of recommendation, which helped induce my client's company to hire him later. The letter, which contained no warning of Allstate's concerns, left Allstate partly liable for his eventual rampage. Eventually, Allstate settled lawsuits stemming from the incident, out of court, for a reported $50 million. Lesson learned: Lack of preparedness and resulting incautious actions can expose you to huge legal consequences.
- **Public relations concerns:** include costs to hire a public relations firm to serve as a media liaison and provide damage control, protect the hard-won, positive associations your company has built over time, and deflect negative media coverage that can significantly damage your reputation.

- **Investor concerns**: include drop in value of stock, the postponement or loss of possible ventures, mergers or other deals, a drop in a firm's credit rating and the loss of analyst confidence. The 1984 chemical leak at a Union Carbide plant in Bhopal, India, was an enormous disaster, resulting in an estimated 3,000 deaths, and 300,000 injuries including blindness and chronic respiratory disease. Soon afterward, facing multiple liability lawsuits—including one for $15 billion—the company's stock price had dropped so that Union Carbide had been devalued by $900 million. The Templeton study mentioned in Chapter Eleven, had this to say about Union Carbide's lack of preparedness, and the resulting costs: "Poor safety measures, the storage of large quantities of lethal gas . . . at the wrong temperature, the accidental or deliberate introduction of water to one of the gas storage tanks, confusion in detecting a rise in pressure in the tank and ineffective response to its detection—all these factors are believed to be responsible for the gas leak tragedy . . . Known costs [to the company], including liability charges and payments to build hospitals, exceed $527,000,000." An otherwise reputable company, Union Carbide experienced the financial costs associated with being unprepared at one point in time.
- **Safety concerns**: include the increased likelihood of accidents both on and off the job following the initial incident, and increased pressure from OSHA or similar regulatory agencies in countries other than the United States. Following the Chernobyl disaster in Russia, the entire nuclear power industry underwent increasing scrutiny by regulators, the media and citizens in communities throughout the world. More recently, the air travel industry has experienced similar scrutiny.
- **Productivity concerns**: include work slowdowns as employees grapple with a difficult situation, downsizing due to a drop-off in business and accidents because of heightened emotions. Lowered morale dampened the Oklahoma Water Resource Board. Located across the street from the Murrah Federal Building, the OWRB building was blown nine inches off its foundation and two people were killed during McVeigh's terrorist blast. The building was closed and people were relocated. The OWRB's administrators reportedly brought in a well-meaning but ineffective Employee As-

sistance Program counselor to run group stress debriefings. Six months later, productivity was still dramatically depressed, absenteeism was up, the work area was disorganized and employees were angry. To their credit, OWRB administrators belatedly took decisive actions to remedy the problem.

- **Outrage**: includes outside reactions to the crisis, such as protesters, sabotage by angry employees and media issues that elicit rage from the public. Laid-off employees can demonstrate this, too. CMI worked with an unprepared company whose laid-off employee encrypted valuable data on the central server, rendering some of it unrecoverable and costing the company over $1 million.

- **Recruiting concerns**: include the prestige of the company. It's difficult to hire new employees at a company associated with a poorly handled disaster. Although studies show that their workers are at no more risk than other industries, many of us associate workplace violence with the U.S. Postal Service. It is safe to assume that this reputation has led to a drop in talented applicants at post offices nationwide.

- **Relationship concerns**: include relationships with customers, suppliers, distributors, stockholders, the media, financial institutions, regulators and others. Compromised relationships can result in lost revenue and negative publicity. A company is no better than its relationships. The financial services company Cantor Fitzgerald lost nearly 700 employees when the World Trade Center was attacked. Cantor CEO Howard Luttnick, shaken with grief, almost immediately announced his intention to "take care" of their families. Days later though, the company removed the lost employees from the payroll, angering many of their families. In the ensuing months, the company did offer specific material help, including extending health insurance coverage and promising to distribute a share of partnership profits to them. It explained that it could not provide such support without a tight focus on its operating budget. While many observers considered this a generous commitment, to others the apparent duplicity felt like a betrayal. Some commentators in the media second-guessed Luttnick's judgment. A good crisis consultant could have helped him safeguard these relationships.

These are just a few of the areas that can ignite in a crisis. They can help you evaluate the severity of your foreseeable risks during your crisis planning process.

The best crisis management is proactive. Preparation helps you respond quickly—and the quicker you take the right actions, the more likely it is that your intervention will succeed.

Quick Use Preparedness Guide

CHAPTER 13: ANALYZING YOUR VULNERABILITIES

- Have you brainstormed possible catastrophic scenarios?
- Have you studied what the ripple effect of vulnerability might be on:
  - Your company
  - Your industry
  - Your customers
  - Your suppliers
  - Your competitors
  - Other relevant audiences?
- Have you further analyzed the likelihood of foreseeable risks using these methods?
  - Query staff
  - Conduct survey
  - Review history
  - Review industry mishaps
  - Assess your location
  - Investigate local crime and labor statistics
  - Conduct online research
- Have you analyzed the severity of each of your foreseeable risks?
- Have you considered the possible negative effects of various disasters on your three core assets?
  - People
  - Finances
  - Reputation
- Have you determined if and how your company could be blamed for each occurrence?

- Have you analyzed these additional areas of severity for each risk?
  - Legal
  - Public relations
  - Investor
  - Safety
  - Productivity
  - Outrage
  - Recruiting
  - Relationships
- Have you used the Probability/Severity Analysis Grid to rank your most likely incidents—and those with the greatest potential for creating severe consequences?

CHAPTER 14

Evaluating Your Existing
Crisis Procedures

Your company succeeds because of its culture, policies, procedures and people. You can build your crisis preparedness on these very same strengths, if you match them to your risks.

Now that you have identified and analyzed the risks of your company, let's move on to the second step in crisis preparedness: evaluation of your existing crisis procedures and controls to address those risks. In this chapter we will discuss:

- How to determine whether your existing response procedures are sufficient for the risks you identified
- How to enhance the capabilities you already have in place

Evaluate Your Existing Strengths

Take a look around your organization. Ask questions of people in the know. What existing strengths and tools can you match against possible catastrophe?

Make a list of the controls that match each foreseeable risk. Some controls will apply to more than one area of vulnerability. For example, a trained, viable Crisis Management Team will apply to every catastrophe. A strong security department and a set of strong procedures will help prevent and respond to many kinds of incidents.

A Tool to Help Evaluate and Enhance Your Strengths

You can use a computer spreadsheet, or a simple table like the one below, to help maintain a clear picture of your preparedness strengths, and your ideas for enhancing them. List your foreseeable risks. Now match them with the policies, procedures and other controls you have in place, keeping in mind that each one might apply to several of the risks you have identified. Then add the enhancements you can make right now. We will discuss developing entirely new controls and procedures in the next chapter; don't worry about the new controls for now.

Foreseeable Risks	Existing Controls	Enhancement of Controls	New Controls
Workplace violence	EAP, guard service	Lower EAP reporting threshold, etc.	Emergency communication plan
Earthquake	Command center, etc.	Additional TVs and recorders	Off-site command center
Loss of critical information	IT manager, backups, etc.	Retain "hacker consultant," etc.	Periodic hacker testing

Leverage Your Strengths to Enhance Preparedness

Leveraging—investing the least amount of time, money and effort, to yield the greatest possible return—always makes good business sense. That's true of preparation for crises as well.

An effective preparedness strategy will require time, money and effort. But, the best investment you can make is in clear thinking. If you don't have a single extra dollar to spend today, you can still make progress by addressing these questions.

TIME

- How soon do you want your preparations to be comprehensive and up-to-date?
- Who in the organization will champion your plan—and how much time should that person realistically devote to the project?
- How many others should be involved, and how much time will the plan demand from each of them?
- How often should the crisis planning committee meet? What investment of time can you expect from senior management?
- How many people will it take to meet the desired deadlines?
- How can you get the greatest result for the least amount of time invested?
- Would an outside consultant, or the benchmarks of other companies, be needed?

MONEY

- Can key points of vulnerability in your defense system be strengthened with minimal, targeted spending?
- How much money is needed for full crisis preparedness?
- What can be done *before* additional financial resources are allocated to improve your preparedness or to better make your case for the needed budget?
- How will your company's investment in crisis planning yield quantifiable savings?

Are there cost-justified enhancements that would better equip your organization to face your identified hazards? You can model an analysis of costs and savings from your own experience, or from that of other organizations. Examine company histories for crises that might have been avoided or better contained. On average, how much did these incidents end up costing? Figure in both hard dollar costs (including lawsuits) and—as best you can—soft costs such as productivity lost to low morale. What amount of money invested to prevent, or respond better to, events like those would have produced a definable degree of savings?

EFFORT—OR, THE INVESTMENT OF HUMAN CAPITAL

- How much effort will your company's culture allow for preparedness efforts?
- Will your people tolerate the minor irritations that can come hand in hand with preparedness, such as extra security checks?
- Is senior management ready to devote enough talented personnel to develop and maintain a crisis preparedness initiative?
- Can the individual members of the crisis planning team depend on their supervisors and coworkers to support their involvement?

Where to Look and What to Look For

Look for lessons in-house. Your company already has a body of experience in responding to and managing unforeseen events. Whether from real disasters it has weathered, or from crisis simulations it has undergone, your company already has a body of experience that can serve as a guide to the future.

When your company has been hit by unexpected turbulence,

- Were the people who took charge and handled your response fully debriefed for lessons learned? Was the information thoroughly analyzed?
- Were the conclusions incorporated into your crisis preparedness plan?
- Was your workforce, in general, solicited for feedback on what had happened?

There may still be gems of insight out there among your workers, just waiting to be mined. Now is a good time to mine them.

If your company has gone through real crises or simulation exercises, but has not thoroughly debriefed the process, now is the time to do so.

You need to know what your company has done right. Also your management team needs to know their crisis response weaknesses in order to establish a reliable preparedness strategy.

One set of resources that is likely to be in place already is your training programs. These may already cover topics such as safety, hostility management and crisis management. In most cases, it will cost little to modify these programs to make sure they address your current situation.

Look for lessons outside. Another way to build on your current strengths is to take a look at the best practices of other organizations.

- How do your plans compare to what other companies have done?
- Are there relatively simple enhancements in place elsewhere that have not occurred to you?

Use the Internet. If you want to retrofit your building to restrict access, for instance, you can get an overview of the products and systems available, and links to professionals who specialize in such work, by searching for phrases such as "security hardware" and "access control system." Other sources you can turn to immediately are the industry and professional associations to which you already belong, and government agencies responsible for public safety and emergency management.

Use local agencies. If you are located in a hurricane or earthquake zone, for instance, you should evaluate your response plans in relation to the latest recommendations of local and state emergency management agencies, and to the plans of emergency response agencies in your area.

Use crisis management consultants. This might be the right time to call in an outside consultant who specializes in crisis management. It wouldn't necessarily take a lot of a consultant's time; a good one should have up-to-date information at his or her fingertips.

Use your insurance broker. Your broker can help you evaluate your existing coverage in light of your expanded risks. Are you carrying adequate insurance, or should your coverage be enhanced? You should also closely examine the crisis response products offered by insurers; they may well include coverage for aspects and effects of disasters that you have not even considered.

Insurers can provide crisis-related coverage for medical and funeral expenses; crisis counseling for grief and trauma victims; travel and temporary living expenses; the costs of securing a site to prevent further damage; for loss of business income; and even for the fees charged by a public relations firm you might hire to help manage your message.

Benchmark other companies' preparedness plans. If there was ever an undertaking ideally suited to benchmarking, crisis preparedness is it. Don't hesitate to approach other companies—even your competitors—to find out how they are handling disaster preparedness. One lesson of September 11, 2001, is that we are all vulnerable.

Painful Lessons: One Example

An explosion a few years ago at a chemical company sent a fireball fifty stories into the air. Debris was blown for ten miles. Over twenty people were killed, and many more injured. This company did an excellent job of implementing its emergency response plan to address the physical content of the crisis. The CEO quickly arrived on-site and did an excellent job as corporate spokesperson, communicating care and compassion for all employees, including those injured and killed and their families. Insurance programs and contingency plans swung into action. The company promised an investigation.

The human side of the crisis was promptly addressed, too. Mental health professionals from a nearby university were called in. Once the fire was out, they reportedly brought in a mobile facility, and positioned it across the street from the explosion site.

But the university personnel were apparently not experienced in crisis intervention. Establishing the counseling offices across the street from the site was a mistake. First, people didn't want their coworkers or managers to see them on their way into counseling. Second, a known symptom of traumatic stress is "avoidance of reminders" of the incident; so having to return to the site for counseling was unacceptable to most. Very few showed up for counseling, despite the good intentions of the providers and management.

Fourteen months later, the company found itself facing more than two hundred lawsuits by victims. One employee—who had not availed himself of the offered counseling in the temporary structure—received a subsequent diagnosis of posttraumatic stress disorder. Company attorneys and the insurer settled the claim for $2 million and required the employee not to divulge the terms of the settlement.

But the employee had a hard time keeping the secret. He "quietly" told his friends from work about his newfound fortune. Within three months, the number of lawsuits swelled to over 1,200 claims—for posttraumatic stress disorder. The exposure from the human side of the crisis, through psychological injury claims, had grown to over $900 million.

Had this company and its provider understood how to structure the post-crisis counseling, the landslide of claims might have easily been avoided. The good news is that your organization need not suffer such consequences to learn from this company's harsh experience.

What You Should Look For: Clear Strategy and Good Tactics

When disaster strikes, you only get one chance to respond. You have to be prepared to do it right—the first time.

You'll go a long way toward ensuring that you are ready, if you critique your plans for clarity as to both strategy and tactics. You need to keep the differences between them clearly in mind—and not mistake one for the other. Your strategy must be a comprehensive plan, and your tactics must be valid and reliable methods of implementation. A valid plan is one that actually accomplishes what it was designed to do. A reliable one can be counted on to work successfully in response to repeated challenges.

Suppose you have identified workplace violence, from a deranged and armed employee for instance, as a possible risk your company faces. In response, your strategy might be to put in place specific systems, like an Employee Assistance Program, and controls, like security guards. The EAP and the guards are tactics you have chosen to address your anti-violence strategy.

But do they amount to a comprehensive strategy? And are they valid tactics—that is, will they really accomplish what you need them to do? Or do they only give you a false sense of security?

Companies often overlook the "people side" of a crisis. And a very common point of confusion between the strategic and the tactical revolves around the EAP. Companies sometimes feel that if they have one in place, they have prepared themselves to handle the people side of any debacle that could arise, including one involving a potentially violent employee.

EAPs are invaluable tools for ensuring the mental health—and thus the morale, satisfaction and productivity—of your workforce. Every company of any size ought to have one. And possibly, if a mental health treatment model is appropriate, counseling may help a threatening individual. But an excellent EAP and security department does not substitute for prepared management strategy and a comprehensive set of controls to address problems like serious threats of violence.

Assessing Strategy and Tactics: One Example

Let's continue with this example, in which the anticipated threat is a violent outburst from a worker, and the mechanisms in place for response are an EAP and security guards.

VALIDITY VS. RELIABILITY

When evaluating your preparedness, you need to consider whether your EAP is truly equipped with reliable and valid elements for your strategy. Do they have professionals who are trained and experienced in handling threats of violence, for instance? Is there a comprehensive and structured management system poised to deal with potentially violent people who are involved in the EAP? Do they have the right skills, such as adequately trained and experienced trauma counselors, with sufficient quality assurance? Will they be in the right place in sufficient quantity, and available to you, in an emergency?

STRATEGY

Strategically, management must offer much more than the EAP. Employee Assistance Program counselors are typically skilled mental health generalists. They may not necessarily be trained in issues of violence, for example. Moreover, confidentiality constraints may prevent them from telling you about a threat. If you anticipate threats of workplace violence, you will need to establish a multidisciplinary Threat Response Team as well as a threat notification system that encourages employees to voice their suspicions of potential violence to the appropriate managers.

If a violent incident does occur, managers, too, must tend to "people issues." They can't pass the buck to the EAP.

A comprehensive strategy for dealing with workplace violence would back up the EAP with broader programs—thus allowing the EAP to focus on the things in which EAP counselors specialize.

TACTICS

And what about that other tactical control you have in place for preventing workplace violence—your security guards? Maybe you feel better knowing that there are uniformed guards in place. But what kind of skills and motivation do your guards really have? Is your guard staff thoroughly familiar with an emergency communication and response plan, in case a threatening individual shows up unexpectedly at your workplace?

We once reviewed the violence preparedness plan for a huge organization that had experienced more than its share of workplace shootings. The receptionists at their various facilities had the following directive listed in their manual to address a gunman (or woman) who showed up at the front lobby: "Keep them occupied and call 911." How many armed perpetrators would sip a cup of coffee and read a magazine while the receptionist called 911? A good plaintiff attorney would have a field day with such a plan.

Whatever your risks, you need a strategy that is clear and comprehensive.

Leave No Strategy or Tactic Unevaluated

Now let's apply this same kind of thinking to some other aspects of crisis preparedness to see whether they are valid and reliable. This is the sort of thorough and methodical process of evaluation you need to do now.

Your organization, for instance, hopefully has designated a person to be in charge of crisis response—capable of handling the task through adequate training and crisis leadership coaching—who is thoroughly familiar with the company's plans. If that person is killed or on vacation at the moment of crisis—will an equally qualified backup person be ready to take over? If not, you have an unreliable control.

What if you were to lose your building? It wouldn't take something as horrendous as a terrorist attack. A fire or hurricane could make your premises unusable. What would you need to get your operations up and running again in temporary quarters? What else would you need in order to keep your people productive? See if your continuity plan needs to be enhanced, to cover all the risks you now recognize. While the tide is changing, most continuity management plans historically have ignored the people-side of recovery.

Now Enhance Your Strengths

How can you build on your company's existing policies, procedures and overall approach to crisis response? By now you should be able to answer the following questions:

- Do our preparedness efforts take into account all the probable and severe events we can foresee?
- Is there a response strategy built into our plans for *every* significant risk?
- Are our crisis prevention and response plans truly valid and reliable? Or are they "false-security" measures that may or may not work?
- Have our policies and procedures been thoroughly communicated to all constituents? Have adequate emergency exercises been conducted?

Still not sure of all the answers? Then this is the time to run crisis simulation exercises. Even if you have held simulations in the past, your fresh analysis of risks, and new skills in mental imagery, make a powerful new lens through which to observe them once again. A procedure that seemed watertight when you practiced it a year ago may have obvious leaks when examined closely now. You will quickly find out which of your existing controls are working and which have noteworthy weaknesses.

You will be leveraging your strengths, and you will see results. This is what crisis-prepared companies do on a regular basis.

Common Elements of Preparedness Plans

Every company's situation is unique. But some elements of preparedness planning are appropriate for nearly everyone. Let's go through a few of them, and look at ways they might be enhanced with very little investment. We'll think of it as a brainstorming session. I know that for every example we look at, you can come up with ideas of your own.

Building security. Every organization must monitor the people who come and go. You might already have a security desk in your lobby at which visitors are asked to check in. If the procedure is not already in place, why not establish an escort policy, by which employees accompany visitors right to their destinations?

Cyber security. Surely your computer systems have virus protection software in place. But are your IT people staying on top of the latest developments in firewall technology? Are you sure that every computer used by your people is protected? What about the machines your employees use when they work from home?

And how secure are your computers from hackers? Have you considered testing your system by hiring a "hacker consultant" to see how easy it might be to get into your system?

Public relations. Your public relations folks probably do a dazzling job of getting out your company's message—during normal times, that is. If they didn't, you would have replaced them long ago. But do you know whether they have the right skills to manage your communications at a time of chaos? To find out, you'll have to ask them the right questions.

Are their people experienced in conducting high-stress, post-crisis press conferences, for instance, when reporters might be aggressively digging for information you are not ready to release? Such a press conference won't be anything like those pleasant events you hold when you launch a product line or announce new members of your board. You need a PR professional who will help you take charge of your image and message, from deciding where your spokesperson should stand to what he or she should communicate if hostile questions arise.

I was involved in a response to a man-made disaster, where the company was blamed for fatalities. The company's outside PR professional was unable to handle the velocity and volume of issues that arose. When it came time for the press conference with the site's senior manager, the PR professional did not find out in advance what questions the media wanted answered. The management spokesperson was thus unprepared for the questions. Moreover, no one briefed him on the message he should have conveyed. The PR professional allowed television cameras to set up outside the building, where they showed the company flag and name clearly. In addition—and potentially most damaging—he allowed people to tell jokes just before the interview so that the cameras captured the image of the manager laughing. Crises demand PR professionals who can cope. The long-term reputation of your organization may depend on its public response. Seemingly small mistakes can cause serious damage to your corporate image.

Company Website. Many proactive companies prepare a crisis-related section to their website, keeping it behind a firewall until it is needed. Such a site might include facts about the company during happier times, its products, executive management, work locations and crisis-specific information. A restaurant chain, for example, may develop background information about exposure to food-borne illnesses like *E. coli.* Such a site provides a way for the media, the public, employees, families and others to easily access useful, positive information about how the company is handling itself. When crisis time hits, you can post the information for public viewing. Daily briefings about when and how the company is responding to the crisis can be regularly updated.

Crisis command center. Many companies have an existing command center. It's time to reevaluate your capabilities here. If you ever actually have to use such a room, you will need it to be furnished with more than a conference table and chairs.

Does the room contain, for example, satellite or cable-connected televisions and VCRs, so that you can monitor and record media coverage? Are adequate telephone and computer lines already in place? You can easily arrange to have additional phone jacks installed now. Then, if the need arises, it will be a simple matter to plug in additional phones, a fax machine and computers with modems. An equally cheap preventative measure is to stock spare chargers for cell phones that team members use; too often, such phones run down during a crisis, while their chargers sit at home.

When considering your Crisis Command Center, remember that in a crisis, your company's phone lines are likely to be jammed. Consider having several lines in the Crisis Command Center with unpublished phone numbers that do not go through the company's normal switching system.

Your organization may not have the luxury of dedicating a large, accessible space solely to crisis management. Think creatively and match your choices to your foreseeable risks. Liberty Mutual, the Boston-based insurance giant, provides an example in point. Because it is not a chemical company or other high-risk operation, its need for a center is statistically small. Yet this progressive company wanted a space that was large, discreet and well equipped. Liberty Mutual's crisis leaders designated a computer training room as their Crisis Command Center.

The room is extremely well suited to its extra purpose. As a training center, it was already equipped with a bank of networked computers, phone outlets and plenty of workspace. It is located in an area of the headquarters building without multiple entrances—so it can be readily secured. For easy reference when the time comes, the company's Corporate Crisis Management Team has created a schematic drawing of the room in its alternative configuration—one that precisely details the crisis layout.

As soon as word comes in that a crisis is underway, designated individuals consult the schematic and within minutes the room is transformed. The same room is used for crisis simulations, a practice that is essential if the command center is to be reliable. Part of the simulation, in fact, involves timing the room conversion to be sure that it falls within an established benchmark.

Despite the large size of the company, Liberty Mutual did not need to overspend to create an excellent Crisis Command Center.

A backup command center location. What if your own building cannot be used? Perhaps there is a nearby hotel where you could plan to set up an off-site command center. But what is in place there to enable you to function in crisis mode? You will want to ask the same questions about communications capability. And you must assess the hotel's security systems. Will there be reliable access control to keep outsiders away from your emergency management operations? You would not want members of the media, for example, walking in on you there unannounced.

And when an emergency arises, what if the room you expect to use at that hotel is booked for some other function? Companies involved in offshore oil extraction in the North Sea know that their industry is a risky one, and they keep themselves prepared for the worst. Many of them expect to run their disaster response efforts from Aberdeen, Scotland. So they have signed contracts with hotels there ensuring that the hotels will pre-empt other functions, if necessary, to give them space for their command centers. The hotels, in turn, include a clause to this effect when they rent function rooms to their everyday clients. Nobody wants to disrupt a wedding reception or retirement party—but an oil-rig explosion deserves precedence.

Keep in mind that any disaster that hits you might hit your neighbors, too. A flood or earthquake could affect many companies in your area. What will happen when response teams and out-of-towners from a dozen other companies show up at the same hotel needing space? Why not get a commitment from the hotel in advance, ensuring that you will get priority?

In this example, your relationship with the nearby hotel is an existing strength. The new terms you work out with the hotel management, for precedence and priority at a time of crisis, would be an effective, inexpensive enhancement you can make right away.

Notification plans. We have discussed earlier how good communication is crucial in any crisis response—especially immediately after an incident. What procedures do you have in place for notifying key individuals that something has occurred? If it's just a list of names and numbers, you should turn it into an Integrated Notification Plan in advance. This would tell you:

- *Who needs to be notified* in each type of incident, and how to alert them
- *What they need to know* to help them act decisively
- *What you need to know from them* in order to effectively manage the crisis

For example, when you call your lawyers to inform them that an explosion has occurred in a part of your plant where chemicals are stored, an *integrated* approach will lead you to ask during the conversation if an attorney should be present, for example, before the incident site is photographed.

An Integrated Notification Plan will help you distinguish between people who "need to know" and those who might "like to know." Many managers may wish to be in the information loop, even if they are not essential players in your response. Your CEO may want to know "immediately, if not sooner" about any calamity—or may be willing to let the senior management team handle most events. Under what circumstances should your board of directors be alerted? Should every member be notified, or only certain ones? The plan should also contain instructions about how to make these notifications. Does the CEO want to be alerted directly from site management, for example, or only through a senior manager?

How much, if at all, should you investigate before you make notification calls?

One top chemical company executive insists on being informed of any type of explosion within ten minutes. He cannot forget the experience of his counterpart at another chemical firm. When that firm suffered a major blast, how do you think the counterpart found out? It was when he answered his door in his bathrobe at 3:00 A.M., and was met with reporters' shouting questions. The plant manager had decided to investigate the incident before reporting it to corporate in order to cover himself—or so he thought!

We have discussed many ways to identify your strengths and enhance what you already have in place. In the next chapter, we will address any gaps or weaknesses you have uncovered, and talk about how to devise new procedures to resolve them.

Quick Use Preparedness Guide

CHAPTER 14: EVALUATING YOUR EXISTING CRISIS PROCEDURES

- Leverage your existing strengths as you plan your response to newly identified risks.
- Use a spreadsheet to evaluate:
  - How your existing plans match up to your foreseeable risks
  - The simple enhancements you can make right now for a small amount of time and money
- Consider what your organization is willing and able to invest in preparedness, in terms of:
  - Time
  - Money
  - Effort
- Look in-house, for the insights and experience your people already have about the dangers you face and the corresponding controls you have in place to prevent them or respond effectively.

- Look outside for help.
  - Check with consultants, specialists like your insurance broker, and government emergency management agencies.
  - Benchmark what other companies are doing.
- Think clearly about strategy and tactics. Is your preparedness strategy comprehensive? Are the tactics it will use valid and reliable?
  - Validity means that the plan actually accomplishes what it was designed to do.
  - Reliability means that it will work successfully under repeated applications.
- Run simulation exercises to test your existing plans against your newly understood risks.
- Consider integrating your notification plan to answer:
  - Who needs to be notified
  - What they need to know
  - What you need to know from them

CHAPTER 15

Identifying New Procedures for Preparedness

The next step is to identify the gaps in your preparedness plan, and design controls for minimizing them.

In this chapter, we will walk through:

- Identifying the risks for which you are not fully prepared
- Developing the procedures that can handle them

Given what you've already accomplished, identifying your weaknesses should not be hard. By now, most of them will be obvious. These are simply the foreseeable risks for which you do not have a comprehensive prevention or response strategy.

Your goal is a crisis preparedness plan that is comprehensive and watertight. This is the step when we find the leaks and plug them.

A "control" is anything you put in place to deal with a specific foreseeable risk. Policies, procedures, methods and management systems can all be thought of as controls. Some controls can apply to—or, control for—more than one foreseeable risk. Others are custom-tailored specifically for a single risk.

Let's take as an example the potential risks that could arrive with your incoming mail. You're certainly aware by now of incidents of terrorism that made use of the mail system. There were the explosive devices sent by the Unabomber, targeted to various corporations. And anthrax was mailed to government and media offices, starting in late 2001. So you incorporated this awareness into the list of possible risks your company could face, back when you were conducting the analysis step of the Six-Step Preparedness Plan.

Now what?

What's the State of the Art?

One way to address your weakness is by benchmarking—that is, investigating the controls already put in place by other organizations. You should look at other companies in your industry. Presumably, you have common perils, since you run similar operations.

But don't fail to look at other kinds of organizations, too. If you face hazards that have to do with geography, like earthquakes or storms, you would want to benchmark the controls of other companies in your locale. If your executives routinely travel to certain unstable parts of the world, you should find out what controls other companies whose people visit the same places use, regardless of their line of business.

Use all the benchmarking resources we discussed in Chapter Fourteen: industry organizations, government agencies, surveys, consultants and managers at other companies. You will then have to decide whether you want to implement the procedures you uncover, devise your own variations of them—or do neither.

Brainstorming New Controls

To identify the new controls you need, start out by brainstorming. You could have the members of your Crisis Preparedness Committee begin the process individually. First, prepare a list of weaknesses. Then, have each member suggest controls for each one. Now, you can consolidate these ideas.

As you brainstorm, consider all the possible responses that could apply to the new risks—even if, at first, some might not appear to fit your culture or budgetary capabilities. As you do this, creative ideas and alternatives will begin to flow. The best way to establish priorities is to put all options on the table.

Imagining the Worst—and Controlling It

Use the imagery technique we have discussed before. This time, instead of simply trying to picture disaster scenarios as they unfold, add a dimension to the exercise. Picture not only what could happen, but what controls might prevent it from happening, or moderate its impact. You want to come up with concrete ways to prevent the ripple effect. For each new risk, ask yourselves:

- What sequence of events might unfold?
- How might each element of the scenario ripple out to other areas?
- What could stop this cascade of related events, at each point in its unfolding?
- What would each affected constituent want in the situation?
- What policies and procedures would offer that protection?

Suppose you are doing this imagery exercise about a situation in which anthrax gets into your building via the mail. Two employees are infected. A hazardous materials team says your building must be shut down for at least three weeks for decontamination. What might different constituents want from you?

- Infected employees: the financial support of their salaries; trauma counseling; and complete medical care. Expect these employees to ask pointed questions about what management did, or did not do, to prevent this exposure
- Their families: trauma counseling; full disclosure of what is known; what to do about items brought home from work that could contaminate them
- Other employees: prompt testing for exposure; full disclosure regarding management's actions; counseling to address fears; continued salary; assurance of job security; measures to prevent further contaminations
- Customers: timely warning about business disruptions; assistance in getting tested, if any exposure is suspected; notification regarding the resumption of normal operations; a response plan to en-

sure the safety of on-site customers and those who receive materials from your company
- Suppliers: notification of alterations in needed supplies, delivery scheduling and the like
- Stockholders: assurance that preparations and actions are adequate to maintain profitable operations; full disclosure of suspected impact on sales and profitability
- Postal inspectors and law enforcement: full cooperation in protecting evidence and assistance in investigations; access to pertinent records that could provide clues
- Other companies in your industry: timely disclosure about incident; any evidence that indicates the possibility of further attacks on related companies
- News media: cooperation and full disclosure about the incident, without jeopardizing the investigation by law enforcement and postal inspectors

Extend this scenario to look for all the possible consequences. How would this anthrax exposure affect your company's

- Reputation?
- Financial condition?
- People?
- Culture?
- Industry?
- Community?
- Business operations?
- Recruiting efforts?
- Insurability?

In this imagery exercise, express every appropriate possibility you can imagine. Of course, in the real event, you can't provide every constituency with everything it might want. There will be conflicting interests between some. Your stockholders, for instance, may be concerned with getting operations back to normal and limiting the costs, while employees and their families may be much more interested in staying home until costly mailroom security measures are implemented. The media may want to know how other companies can protect themselves from what happened to you.

Meanwhile, your security department is interested in hiding your remaining weaknesses.

The Reasonable Person Test

What if a procedure is used in your industry or neighborhood, or by businesses in general—and you decide *not* to use it? You should clearly document why you considered it, and why you decided not to use it—in a manner that would pass the "reasonable person" test. This documentation should be constructed during the planning process. After an incident has occurred, it's too late.

Consider the situation of All-Tech Investments, the day-trading company with offices in our corporate headquarters building in Atlanta, where Mark Barton went on the shooting spree I described in the introduction of this book. Benchmarking could have told All-Tech that many firms housed in Atlanta's financial district were installing sophisticated card-swipe security systems to control access to their offices. But as a regular trader at that office, Mark Barton would have had open access—so such a system would not have stopped him. In addition, a system like that would feel unfriendly to existing and potential day-trading customers. In this case, All-Tech could have documented that it looked at this new system because many offices in its building were installing one, but the company determined that it would be neither practical to use, given the nature of the services the company provides to the public, nor effective against a disgruntled trader or employee. Documentation wouldn't keep the company from being sued, but it could help avoid a costly judgment of negligence. Negligence comes into play if a company's failure to prepare, or to act, does not appear to be reasonable.

The reasonable person test:

- Reflects what an informed person would have expected you to do, given what you knew (or should have known) at the time and were capable of doing.
- Recognizes that you are operating in a context that is continually evolving. What is reasonable at one time may appear inadequate and irresponsible if circumstances change.

Let's apply this standard to airline security. Before the first wave of airliner hijackings in the 1970s, there was virtually no control over access to airplanes, other than having a ticket. Neither passenger identification nor baggages were checked. Access to airports was wide open. Since there was no history of terrorism aboard airplanes, this lack of security would have passed a reasonable person's scrutiny at that time.

Once a pattern of hijackings emerged, certain security measures were put in place. Sky marshals rode incognito. Ticket agents silently profiled passengers. Baggage and passengers had to pass through metal detectors, to screen for weapons. The general experience in that period was that even if a hijacking occurred, within a few hours or days the passengers would be free to return home. So, the new security measures seemed adequate. And indeed, hijackings diminished.

Since then, the willingness of terrorists to make use of airliners has escalated. First came bombs hidden in luggage that was stored in a plane's hold, when the perpetrators themselves were not aboard the flight. That's what brought down the Pan Am flight at Lockerbie, Scotland. After that tragedy, a reasonable person would have expected that security measures would screen checked baggage and make sure that no baggage is on board without its owner. More recently, we have seen terrorists willing to commit suicide in order to turn airliners into missiles—a tactic previously unimagined. This method has precipitated many new procedures. With each change in circumstances, the measure of what an informed person would consider reasonable has changed.

Another way to apply the reasonable person test is to evaluate the plausibility of controls in light of simple common sense. Infectious agents sent through the mail are certainly a risk. But would a reasonable person suggest that the Postal Service open every letter and package to make sure it's safe before sending it on its way?

Taking the reasonable person test into consideration will assist you in two ways. First, you will be able to defend your actions against charges of negligence, should you ever be challenged over your prevention, preparedness and post-crisis response efforts. Second, if your actions seem reasonable to those who are affected, they are more likely to cooperate. For example, prior to the terrorism of 2001, it would have seemed unreasonable to passengers to submit themselves to the scrutiny that has been implemented since. Today however, these security measures seem inconvenient and there is grumbling, but the measures seem reasonable to the common person.

The Darker Side of "Reasonable"

The reasonable person test seems simple and logical, doesn't it? Now allow me to take the gloves off and knock you around for a minute. I want you to imagine what might happen if you fail to do what could be considered reasonable.

Suppose you did not conduct a thorough risk analysis, leaving your company vulnerable to risks you should have foreseen. Or maybe you did start to work a preparedness plan. You identified possible new controls for the areas in which your plans were weak. But then for some reason—cost or lack of commitment from management—you did not follow through and put these new controls in place.

Then, an event you could have foreseen comes to pass—with devastating consequences.

What kind of grilling would you get in court from a plaintiff attorney pursuing a liability claim, if the attorney can show that you knowingly allowed the disaster to occur?

"The best example is Pan Am 103," says James Kreindler, partner in the law firm Kreindler and Kreindler. He served as plaintiff attorney in suits arising from such high profile airline disasters as TWA 800, Swissair 111, Egyptair 990 and Pan Am 103—which blew up over Lockerbie, Scotland, in 1988, after taking off from Frankfurt.

"Every airline has an Air Carrier Standard Security Procedure, that sets forth the rules for their security system, whether they do it themselves or hire outside contractors," Kreindler explains. "Pan Am's ACSSP required the positive match of passengers to baggage for interline passengers—those connecting to Pan Am from another airline—at extraordinary security airports, which included Frankfurt. Positive match means making sure that a passenger who has actually gotten on the airplane accompanies each bag.

"The regulation said, 'When you find an unaccompanied bag, the airline must either not carry it, or carry it only if it can be opened and physically inspected.'

"Pan Am, in 1988, was losing money and cutting costs. The emphasis in every department was to cut costs. They purchased a few X-ray machines and started X-raying interline bags. Pan Am's security manager in London wrote to corporate headquarters in New York, and said, 'The rules require positive match. We're X-raying interline bags. Do we still have to match them?' And corporate headquarters wrote back, 'No, just load them and go,' thus saving all that money from the cumbersome passenger match.

"So it was this corporate decision that caused the Lockerbie disaster, because the bomb was in an unaccompanied interline bag transferred to the Pan Am plane, in Frankfurt, from Air Malta. That is probably the clearest, classic example of how cutting corners with security or safety is going to cause a disaster. And in fact, in Pan Am's bankruptcy petition in 1990, the first reason they cited for the bankruptcy was the Flight 103 case," and the likelihood that the airline would have to pay enormous damages.

If you're the plaintiff attorney in a case like this, Kreindler says, "in court, you just rip them to pieces." If you had been in charge of the airline's security during this incident and were cross-examined in court, here's how it might go:

ATTORNEY: "You're in charge of security, and that means following the ACSSP to prevent hijacking and bombing?"

DEFENDANT: "Yes."

ATTORNEY: "And those rules are there to help prevent disasters such as Lockerbie?"

DEFENDANT: "Yes."

ATTORNEY: "And prevent the deaths of all your passengers?"

DEFENDANT: "Yes."

ATTORNEY: "And you didn't do a positive match, did you?"

DEFENDANT: "No."

ATTORNEY: "The reason you didn't provide the ACSSP required baggage check is because it was too expensive, correct?"

DEFENDANT: "Yes."

You never want to be asked such questions in a courtroom. The jury would hate you. And what about discussing, but not implementing, a possible control that turns out to have been needed? "That's what makes out intentional wrong-doing or willful misconduct," says Kreindler. "It's that kind of intentional disregard that exposes you to punitive damages."

If you do all you can now to prevent disaster, you can go a long way to en-

suring that you will never face a courtroom grilling like the one Kreindler
gave Pan Am's managers.

Primary vs. Secondary Prevention

As you identify new controls, you must consider the two types of prevention: primary and secondary.

The point of primary prevention is to keep unwanted incidents from
happening in the first place. This is the approach commonly taken by
safety and security managers. Physical security, safe travel policies and
safety programs all address primary prevention. Primary prevention is essential, but it's not enough.

In spite of your best efforts, bad things will happen. Secondary prevention measures are established to stop a critical situation that has already occurred from escalating—that is, to prevent the ripple effect of vulnerability.

Managers many times concentrate on primary prevention so much that
they get tunnel vision about what could really unfold in a crisis. Recently, I
was involved in a rescue mission for seven employees of three oil-related
companies who had been kidnapped for ransom in the jungles of Ecuador.
Such kidnappings are frequent in Colombia and Ecuador, so it's appropriate to focus energy on prevention, but beyond the services that were provided by negotiators from insurance companies, secondary prevention was
inadequately prepared. Secondary prevention in this kind of situation involves issues such as:

- Negotiations for a quick and safe release of hostages. In this situation, one of the seven hostages was killed; his body was left on the
  side of a road with a written demand for money and threats against
  the others.
- Assistance for traumatized Ecuadorian-national employees who
  were held at gunpoint as the Americans were taken hostage. In this
  case, they had been threatened with death when they refused to say
  where two Americans had hidden.
- Assistance for those two Americans who narrowly escaped kidnap.
- Assistance for the employees in Quito, Ecuador, where oil-rig
  workers are hired and dispatched into the field. It is common for

these headquarters personnel to feel guilty, and to feel concerned for their own safety, knowing that employees, and possibly family members, of the company are being targeted.

- Support for the families of those who had been kidnapped; the families felt helpless. They needed information and qualified trauma counseling. Desperate family members could have made the situation worse by arriving on-site, meddling in negotiations or making public appeals to companies to pay more money.

- Then there is the media involvement. In this case, after one hostage was killed, Bryant Gumbel twice invited family members of a hostage to appear on CBS' *The Early Show*. Gumbel served as an antagonist leading the cry that the involved companies were valuing ransom money more highly than the lives of the kidnapped employees. There is a delicate balance; an offer of money often leads kidnappers to raise the stakes.

- Upon release, after more than 140 days, the hostages needed personal assistance in many arenas, including medical treatment for malnutrition, tropical diseases and infestations. Emotionally, they were at risk of posttraumatic stress disorder.

- There was a need for a well-planned reentry into society and reintroduction to their families. The released hostages didn't sleep well for several nights, even though they were able to sleep in clean beds for the first time in months.

- There were a myriad of other issues. I had the duty of notifying the hostages that the kidnappers had killed their friend, because as we had suspected, the hostages had been led to believe he had been released as a goodwill gesture. It was also important to protect the ex-hostages from the media. There was a need for re-entry back to work for those who chose to stay in their same positions.

Prevention is best, but preparedness for the secondary implications of a crisis is also paramount. It's terribly important to establish controls for secondary prevention. Your company must continually ask itself:

- If this foreseeable situation were to occur, how should we respond?
- What could be done to keep an incident from cascading into a full-blown catastrophe?

These questions apply both to the tangible content of a crisis, and to the intangible impact it could have on your people. Consider these examples of primary and secondary prevention:

Type of Incident	Primary Prevention	Secondary Prevention
Kidnapping for ransom in foreign country	All personnel to be routinely escorted by security guards	Evacuation plan for all remaining personnel, in the event anyone is kidnapped
Workplace violence perpetrated by disgruntled former employee	Threat Response Team, and enhanced physical security at premises	Trauma counseling for employees and family members
Fire or explosion at plant	State-of-the-art containment technology, and frequent safety checks for all volatile materials	Sprinkler system throughout building, and evacuation plan with regular practice drills
Earthquake	All facilities to meet or exceed latest earthquake-zone building codes	Backup electrical generation and data storage capacities
Anthrax exposure from incoming mail	Strict mailroom screening of incoming mail, before distribution	Bio-bags available to all employees for use in containing suspected contaminated letters

Bringing It Down to Earth: Identifying Controls You Need in Place

By encouraging you to brainstorm, I am not forgetting that you operate in a real world of constraints. In a crisis, you will want to respond to every appropriate need. And all your constituents will want you to respond to their needs, too. Let's agree that you can't do it all. So it is up to you, now, to match the range of primary and secondary prevention controls with:

- What is possible, given your budget and culture
- What is reasonable, given what you have determined about the probability and severity of your foreseeable hazards
- The achievable controls that, taken together, would give you the most comprehensive preparedness strategy

In the next several chapters, we will examine ways to organize and prioritize the elements of your preparedness strategy, how to phase them in over time in a way that does not overwhelm your company's resources, and how to keep your plans tuned and poised for quick, complete responses as needed.

Quick Use Preparedness Guide

CHAPTER 15: IDENTIFYING NEW PROCEDURES FOR PREPAREDNESS

- What weaknesses have emerged as you analyzed your foreseeable risks and evaluated your existing strategy?
  - ○ What controls can you devise to address each weakness?
- Have you benchmarked potential controls with:
  - ○ others in your industry?
  - ○ others in your locale?
  - ○ others who share similar risks?

- Have you researched current preparedness standards through
  - industry associations?
  - the Internet?
  - government emergency management agencies?
  - crisis consultants?
  - others
- Has your Crisis Preparedness Committee brainstormed new controls?
  - Have you used imagery exercises to predict the ripple effect of vulnerability that could occur with each foreseeable danger?
  - Have you considered what each of your constituents would want/need/expect in each type of crisis?
  - Have you considered how each type of crisis could affect your company's reputation, financial condition, business operations, people, culture, industry and community?
- Have you subjected your overall crisis preparedness to the reasonable person test?
  - If you have discarded some ideas for prevention or post-incident response, is your documented reasoning clear and defensible?
- Have you prepared adequately for both primary and secondary prevention?
  - For each foreseeable risk scenario, have you allowed for controls that would provide crisis prevention *and* post-crisis response?

CHAPTER 16

Organizing Your Plan

In the previous chapters, we have looked at ways to analyze your foreseeable risks, evaluate your current level of preparedness, and identify the controls you need to add—"A," "E" and "I."

Now it's time for "O." In this chapter, we will discuss what you must do to organize the material you have developed so far.

Organizing for crisis preparedness need not intimidate you any more than any other project you undertake. It just calls upon you to apply the skills you already use in your business life every day—like prioritizing tasks, communicating intentions, eliciting support, executing actions and documenting what you have done.

You have evaluated your current preparedness, and identified the new controls you must establish in order to have a comprehensive plan. Now let's see how to make that comprehensive plan a fixture of your company's culture.

Consider the Whole System

No action you take, or policy or procedure you establish, will exist in a vacuum. You must consider how each new control might affect and be affected by the system as a whole. Some plans that look good on their own can cause systemic problems. And the system is not limited to what goes on within your organization. It includes the context in which your company operates, as well.

An example of a systemic problem coming from a preventive control can be seen right now in Ecuador. Because of increasing guerrilla activity, and frequent incidents of violence and kidnapping, oil companies working in Ecuador began hiring units of the Ecuadorian military to protect their sites. In so doing, they enticed poorly paid soldiers away from border patrol duties. Now, it is easier than ever for guerilla groups to infiltrate from Colombia, putting the oil companies at greater risk than before.

Before you implement any new control, ask:

- What might its possible impact be on other systems within and around our organization?
- What negative consequences may arise from doing this?

To answer these questions, I suggest you again use the techniques of imagery to envision the sequence of possible events.

No Company Is an Island

Suppose you have a warehouse operation on the Mississippi River in southern Louisiana. You have determined that in the next ten years there is a high probability that this region will be hit by a major hurricane.

Also, among your industrial neighbors are oil refineries and chemical and plastics plants. Some of them have abysmal safety records. So you have concluded that there is a high probability that there could be a leak or explosion at one of these places, and that the effect on your operations could be quite severe, including injuries or even fatalities.

You can't control the weather. But it's relatively simple to minimize its impact. You can educate your workers to heed evacuation warnings, which would go some distance toward ensuring that nobody is killed. You can encourage them to keep emergency supply kits in their cars during hurricane season, so that if they do have to evacuate, the experience will be less grueling for them and their families. You can make sure your warehouses are engineered to withstand high winds. And you can buy insurance to cover storm damage to your property and inventory.

What can you do about the risk from those unreliable neighbors?

You could furnish your own facility with hazardous materials equipment, like gas masks and decontamination showers, and train your workers in their use. You can install engineering controls that may help, such as a culvert around your perimeter to route away any spilled liquids. You can establish good communications with local regulators and the managers of the neighboring companies, to ensure that you will be quickly alerted in the event of any dangerous leak.

What you cannot do is get inside your neighbors' organizations to repair whatever management flaws are responsible for their worrisome safety records. Your company and theirs, after all, are unrelated. And each of you is a player in a free-market economic system, in which each entity makes its own decisions.

You could, however, as a corporate citizen of your community—and in your own self-interest—raise the issue of safety. You could do this informally, in conversation with your counterparts from these companies on the golf course. Or you could decide to call publicly for enhanced regulation and more frequent inspection by environmental and industrial regulators.

But meddling in another company's operations, or encouraging more regulation, may go against your own company's grain. If you did manage to agree among yourselves to take that sort of step, you would need to develop political skills different from those needed to install hurricane straps to your warehouse roof.

It may be more comfortable to move your warehouse to another location, even at great expense. But if a dangerous leak from a neighboring plant is a probability, you really have to do *something* to control for it.

Getting Prepared Can Challenge Your Culture

Some preparedness measures can be costly, requiring investments in equipment and the hiring of extra personnel. Such measures can be a tough sell if your company has always prided itself on a lean-and-mean style.

Preparedness may mean sacrificing things of which you are justly proud—such as the architectural qualities of a building. Kansas City International Airport is an example of a once-great building that no longer works well—simply because times have changed. Planned before the era of airliner hijackings, KCI's layout provided parking and a separate entrance near every gate, allowing travelers to board planes with little wasted time. Sadly, security requirements have long since closed some entrances, and necessitated costly screening checkpoints at others. KCI is now as unwieldy as any other airport.

Preparedness means recognizing that even organizations involved in apolitical or even beneficial activities—from universities to department stores to manufacturers of pharmaceuticals—can be in danger.

CMI once set up a crisis-preparedness system for a large international retailer, whose CEO is a devout Christian. He firmly believes that God will watch over the company, making preparations unnecessary. He did allow us to implement some prevention and response measures, but has refused any personal crisis leadership coaching—an important part of any program. If the CEO and senior management are not personally prepared for crises, the whole organization can suffer. So far, the retailer has experienced only moderately severe incidents. But it is best not to rely on luck, however divinely inspired.

There can also be cultural resistance at the field level. CMI helped a *Fortune* 500 company to develop and implement a violence-prevention program. One policy requires managers to confront employees who make threats. One manager decided that was asking too much. "There is no way I'm going to confront a guy we know about who has made threats," he said. "Corporate can tell us to do it, but they don't have to live in the same neighborhood with this guy after he's fired." (It is important to address the managers' desire to be seen as sympathetic to workers. In this case, we recommended that the manager who does the confrontation explain to the dangerous employee that even though they don't want to have this confrontation, they have been forced to do so by an unnamed outside attorney.)

Anticipating Resistance and "Smoothing in" New Controls

Even those of us who believe we're surfing the wave of the latest innovations in technology and business can resist change. And if individuals can drag their heels, organizations can sometimes dig in like balky mules.

Imagery, the technique we discussed earlier, can help you anticipate the resistance you may encounter.

This time, use the ideas you chose in Chapter Fourteen and the new controls you came up with in Chapter Fifteen, as you ask yourself:

- What hurdles do you need to overcome?
- Who needs to be brought on board to ensure success?

- Who will be responsible for this control's ongoing effectiveness?
- What new procedures would have to be established?
- What routines in the organization would have to be modified or replaced?
- What points of resistance might you encounter once the control is in place?
- Which departments and fields of operation will be affected by the new controls?
- Which decision makers' active support could smooth the process?
- Who in the organization has intimate knowledge of the areas you need to change?
- What other kinds of support and materials will be required?
- What costs will be incurred?

Don't Try to Go It Alone

Beware of unilateral implementation of new preparedness controls. It might seem quicker and more efficient. But keep in mind that every member of your organization wants to feel protected. If you establish broad participation, your planning will be many times stronger than it could otherwise be. In fact, with broad support, such planning could contribute to your employees' sense of well-being—and thus to the company's overall productivity. It can also increase the level of comfort among shareholders, financial analysts, the board of directors, lenders, suppliers, franchisees and customers.

Gaining Senior Management Buy-In

As every manager knows, an organization's culture and tone are set at the top. When you must challenge or modify that culture in the name of crisis preparedness, securing the active commitment of top leadership is key. Here's how:

- Show them case histories that could have applied to your organization—with descriptions of how such incidents have affected other companies. Many times, senior managers are unaware of the variety of crises to which the company is vulnerable. A presentation of his information can be compelling. Some crisis consultants maintain a database of information on affected companies, which could furnish raw material for a survey of case histories.

- Establish a budget for your plan, including a cost-benefit comparison to the losses suffered by companies that were unprepared for disasters like the ones you foresee. While you're at it, make the case that crisis preparedness should be an annual budget item equal in importance to insurance and other entrenched risk management methods.
- Provide benchmarking data comparing your organization's preparedness to that of similar organizations.
- Show the information you have gathered from the Department of Labor or other appropriate government entities about the incidents that could affect your organization.
- Your insurer or insurance broker may be willing to share actuarial data that show the risks inherent to your industry and locales that need to be managed.
- Present information from crisis consultants, local law enforcement, FBI, CIA, private security groups or others in the know.
- Public relations firms can compile information about relevant news stories.
- Use some of the information in this book, such as the positive survey results of the Reputation Institute for companies that effectively handled the September 11, 2001, terrorism in Chapter Thirteen. Share the results of the Templeton study on shareholder value from Chapter Eleven. Which category would senior management prefer to be in, the prepared or unprepared?

It also helps to know what gets your decision makers' attention. Are they more convinced by stories about what happened to others in your industry, or are they more statistically oriented? A big part of organizing your plan will involve selling it to senior management.

Monitor, Monitor, Monitor

Your plans must also include the mechanisms for ensuring that new controls are:

- Properly implemented
- Working effectively as planned
- Monitored for quality over time

Without monitoring, even the best-conceived controls can become useless, or worse. Consider this crisis-management debacle:

In the early 1990s, CMI pioneered the first formal family representative training program for the commercial airlines. The program provides assistance for families and surviving passengers of air crash victims through trained employee volunteers.

Unfortunately, one airline ran into trouble with its monitoring.

According to newspaper accounts, the airline assigned a single male family representative volunteer to an unmarried female passenger who had survived a recent crash. Against stated policy, they assigned just one volunteer, rather than two. Moreover, there was apparently no professional supervision of that volunteer. As you might have guessed by now, the family representative had an affair with the crash victim. The airline was sued for negligence and had to pay a large settlement. Proper monitoring can prevent such incidents.

Quick Use Preparedness Guide

CHAPTER 16: ORGANIZING YOUR PLAN

- Have you considered ways that the controls you need may conflict with your company's culture or external environment?
  - ○ Have you anticipated how each control may be received?
  - ○ Have you taken steps to build broad support for your efforts?
  - ○ Have you considered how each control might affect your system as a whole?
- Have you determined:
  - ○ Who will be responsible for each control's ongoing effectiveness?
  - ○ What new procedures or lines of responsibility will have to be established?
  - ○ What routines in the organization will have to be modified?
  - ○ What points of resistance might be encountered?
  - ○ What other kinds of support and materials will be required?

○ What costs will be incurred?

○ Which decision makers' active support could smooth the process of implementing new controls?

○ Where in the organization can you cultivate the support of other individuals?

- Have you estimated an implementation budget for your preparedness plan, including a cost-benefit comparison to the losses suffered by companies that were unprepared?

- Have you prepared a compelling case for senior management?

- Have you built in mechanisms to make sure new controls are properly implemented and monitored?

CHAPTER 17

Utilizing Your Plan

You have analyzed, evaluated, identified and organized your preparedness plans. Now you're ready to utilize them.

Step by Step

Utilizing your preparedness plan means executing a series of distinct steps: You must communicate the plan throughout the organization. The people involved must be trained. They must practice the plan, in drills that will prepare them for actual emergency situations. You must debrief the participants. And then you will want to refine the plan based on what you've learned.

Who Will Utilize Your Preparedness Plan?

Utilizing your plan requires you to establish a working group, and to name leaders. Typically, crisis-prepared companies set up:

- Crisis Response Leaders at key levels and locations within the organization
- A Crisis Management Team, or several teams at strategic points in your organization's structure

The crisis management team. The membership of your Crisis Management Team could include some of the same individuals who served on your

Crisis Preparedness Committee. By now, those people will certainly be familiar with your anticipated risks and needs. But you now need other qualities, too. For one thing, your members must be generally available. They should be able to remain cool under pressure. They should be capable of decisive action and good judgment even when information is incomplete.

You want a team that is multidisciplinary, not only in terms of expertise, but also in terms of personality. Include people who are action-oriented, as well as creative thinkers who can generate solutions. And choose people who are skilled at working in a group.

Depending on your resources, you might even want to invest in the development of the team through techniques like group retreats, wilderness challenges and the like. In any case, team members must be thoroughly trained in your preparedness and response plans.

In a large organization, you will probably need to establish many teams, at various levels and sites. Each should follow a consistent methodology.

Your Crisis Management Team's structure will depend on your size, the number of critical incidents you anticipate per year, your geographic locations and the management philosophy of your company. Some companies prefer to have a centralized CMT, typically at the corporate level, that may be mobilized often enough to keep its members' skills at optimal levels. You may also opt for decentralized Crisis Management Teams, who know the local customs and people.

In many large corporations, the corporate team mobilizes only when an incident hits a defined threshold. Expected financial losses of a given value—say, more than $100,000—would activate the corporate team. Anything less than that would be handled locally.

The same system can be utilized in smaller organizations, with defined thresholds to trigger the involvement of different management levels. Threshold levels may be defined by:

- Financial exposure
- Serious injury or deaths
- Level of media coverage (local, national or international)
- Blame or charges of negligence directed toward management
- Business disruption
- Incidents exceeding insurance deductibles
- Recurring incidents

- Anticipated OSHA, EPA or other government investigations
- Investor relations concerns
- Involvement of contractors, franchisees, distributors, suppliers or other outsiders
- Incidents with anticipated legal disputes
- Compromised security
- Incidents defined or named by senior management

Crisis response leaders. While your Crisis Planning Committee champion served to provide motivational leadership, the response leaders you identify now should be thought of more as point people. They should be placed at each location where you expect to need a crisis response capability. These are the people who must provide critical leadership in the event of a real disaster.

The Right Mix Makes a Stronger Team

When first learning of a calamity, most of us have similar initial reactions. Our hearts beat faster. Our palms go clammy. We feel a wave of nausea.

But our lasting reactions are more individualized. We each have a *stress style* that emerges under times of great pressure. Understanding your personal stress style and those of your team members puts you in a stronger position to capitalize on strengths and compensate for weaknesses, when you and your team members are under pressure. Analyzing the stress styles of all the possible candidates for your Crisis Management Team helps you to pick the right mix of individuals and build a resilient group.

Use the following matrix to determine your typical style in normal, daily living, social and professional situations by using this simple two-step process:

1. On the center horizontal line that separates *Less Assertive* and *More Assertive* plot your common daily living style. The way you operate every day—the way others think of you. If you move toward people easily and have no trouble speaking your mind or promoting your ideas, you would fall on the *More Assertive* side of the continuum. If you are one who waits to be asked questions, and are less forceful in your dealings with others, plot yourself

Task Oriented

Methodical and Analytical	Controlling and in Command
Agreeable and Team Player	Communicative and Animated

Less
Assertive

More
Assertive

People Oriented

closer to the *Less Assertive* side. Where do you rank yourself on the assertiveness line?

2. On the center vertical line, plot whether you tend to be more task-oriented or have a more "people" orientation. For example, does getting the job done take precedence over relationships? People who are highly task-oriented tend to be less interested in those around them and more interested in achievements. Those who are highly people-oriented consider their relationships with others of greater importance than the tasks themselves. Plot yourself on the people vs. task-oriented line.

3. If you rank yourself as task-oriented and less assertive, your personality style tends to be methodical and analytical. If you are task-oriented and more assertive, you tend to be controlling and in command. If you lean toward people-oriented and less assertive, your typical pattern is agreeable and a team player. And, if you are people-oriented and more assertive, your personality style is inclined to be communicative and animated.

Obviously, this is a broad-strokes exercise, not a precise personality profile. No one is completely assertive or completely passive. And, as you know from your own experience, those who move through personal and professional life successfully tend to strike a balance between all these tendencies. What's useful here is to gain a general insight into your traits or style.

"Analysis Paralysis" and Other Tendencies

Now, look at this next matrix and notice the "stress style," which shows the tendency for each of the personality styles under significant stress. If you find yourself in the *Methodical/Analytical* category, you are a thorough and dependable worker who makes few errors. Your strengths include the ability to attend to details and plod through to accomplish tasks. However, you may tend to avoid quick, decisive decisions under stress. It's a tendency called "analysis paralysis."

Task Oriented

Methodical and Analytical Stress Style: *Avoiding*	Controlling and in Command Stress Style: *Autocratic*
Agreeable and Team Player Stress Style: *Submissive*	Communicative and Animated Stress Style: *Disapproving*

Less Assertive   More Assertive

People Oriented

If this sounds like you under fire, think about compensating. In a crisis, you may need to push beyond your normal tendency to be methodical, even when you may only have partial knowledge and what seems like too little time to weigh choices carefully. There are times when waiting to act can make a situation worse.

If you identified yourself as *Controlling/in Command,* you are one who pushes projects through with speed and determination. You're recognized for your ability to take charge. But your stress style may be to become autocratic. Under stress, such people (and they include many top CEOs and other hard-driving, successful types) find it hard to listen. They want to make something happen, regardless of the possible consequences.

If this is your penchant, think about tempering it during a crisis by gathering input from a multidisciplinary group before acting. Listen to others' viewpoints. Take the time to gather sufficient information before taking decisive action.

If your style is *Agreeable/Team Player* you are an all around "nice person" who gets along with others and excels at team building. Your strengths lie in mediating, listening and gaining consensus. But when it hits the fan, your may tend to give in to others. Under stressful conditions you tend to avoid rocking the boat. So your valuable ideas may go unheard. To reduce this possibility, work harder to express your viewpoints, even if they conflict with those of others.

If you ranked yourself in the *Communicative/Animated* category, know that your interpersonal strengths are a valuable asset that can be used to motivate others. You readily supply creative ideas and useful solutions to problems. But when chaos looms, you may become disorganized. Your motivation may diminish if others don't readily adopt your ideas. As stress mounts, you may become critical of others. Remember that not everyone moves as quickly as you do. Respect their need to be methodical.

A team approach that melds all the styles is a good defense against chaos. By becoming aware of the strengths and stress styles of yourself and others, you can balance the personalities on your team in a way that will accelerate resolution.

Develop a Schedule for Utilizing Your Plan

Some parts of your plan may be relatively quick and easy to put forward. For instance, instructions for building evacuation procedures can be communicated to and exercised by your entire workforce in a short time. Still, overall, it will take time to put your comprehensive plan in place and test it for effectiveness—perhaps even a period of a few years.

As with any big project, you will have to prioritize its elements, and establish a schedule for its implementation. You should clearly document the schedule you set. If a crisis occurs before your plan is fully in place and tested, or at some location you have not yet prepared, this documentation can serve as proof of your intentions. It can help you pass the "reasonable person" test if your company is later accused of negligence.

HARDWARE

You will need to explicitly set out your crisis-response policies and procedures in a manual. The Crisis Management Team needs to have this information during training and drills—and, of course, in the event of the real thing.

You have some options when it comes to publishing the manual. Should you publish it in hard copy only? File it on your company intranet? Put it into handheld electronic organizers?

The physical ways you maintain your plan should fit your company's culture and personality. Handheld organizers, for example, are efficient. In a sales or accounting department, where many employees are familiar with them, they might seem to be just the way to go. But the managers in your factories, who may be less comfortable using such devices, might find them frustrating in a high-pressure situation—and might forget to keep them charged, rendering them useless.

Distribute your crisis manual in a way that works for your organization, and makes the information accessible to everyone who needs it.

SOFTWARE

You want your people to understand that a workable plan is in place. You want each of them to know what actions might be expected of them. You want all your employees to be aware of risks, and what they can do to minimize them.

Communicating your plan is an internal public relations challenge. Its goal should be twofold. Ultimately, everyone in the organization should buy in to the idea of preparedness. And, all should recognize that management takes seriously the risks to the company and to its individuals. The benefits will be enhanced preparedness and better morale.

Training . . . and Practice . . . and More Practice

In the event of any critical occurrence, the members of your Crisis Management Team will have to work smoothly, in a group, under enormous pressure. You need to train them well.

Your crisis response manual. Your manual should cover only genuine responses. A common mistake made in the preparation of these manuals is to write them as "training documents." Of course you will use your manual in the course of training. But in a real crisis, your team members will not want to use a manual that is sprinkled with training exercises or long paragraphs.

Another common error is to tell readers what they *should* have done to prepare. In the heat of a crisis, it is too late to harangue people about uncompleted to-do lists.

THREE DEGREES OF SIMULATION

You should run three kinds of exercises with your team: tabletop exercises, simulation exercises, and activation and notification drills.

Tabletops are non-threatening and non-dynamic. They are meant to provide your crisis team with experience in the details and operation of your plan—but in a learning environment, without time pressure.

Simulations are real-time, dynamic improvisations of crisis conditions. Their purpose is to identify strengths and areas that need improvement in your plan and your team—in elevated-tension conditions that closely resemble those of a genuine crisis.

Activation and notification exercises involve assembling the team as quickly as possible, regardless of the nature of the crisis.

DEVELOPING SCENARIOS FOR
EXERCISES AND SIMULATIONS

Both successful tabletop exercises and simulations require disaster scenarios that are serious. One common design failure is to pose a challenge that is insufficiently realistic or too small to hold your team's attention.

None of the participants should learn the content of the
vance. To ensure an engaging scenario, the simulation de
meet privately with managers who will not be involved i
Every aspect of the story must be challenging, realistic and b

On the other hand, it is possible to overwhelm a team—especially one
that is newly formed—by introducing something that is too elaborate,
complex or fast moving. Designing simulations is an exacting, detailed
task. As you prepare one, ask yourself these questions:

- Does the scenario fully utilize the content of your crisis manual
  and elements of your preparedness plan?
- Are there challenges incorporated into the scenario that will exercise and test (but not overwhelm) every discipline represented on
  your crisis management team—such as legal, human resources, security, public relations and all the others?
- Is the scenario sufficiently realistic that it will engage team members, and thus serve as a real preparation?

The consultant we call on most for such exercises likes to prepare by
reading Dean Koontz and Stephen King novels. "That's the level of intri-
cacy and detail—and emotional tension—I want to achieve in an exercise,"
he says.

These exercises are critical to your preparedness. Designing them properly takes an elaborate set of skills. Many companies find it useful to hire a
specialist.

TABLETOP EXERCISES

A tabletop exercise is a scheduled meeting that takes place in a conference
room or Crisis Command Center. Using a discussion-based approach, a
tabletop exercise introduces a team (or teams) to crisis management concepts. No equipment is involved, and all activity occurs inside the meeting
room.

The exercise leader begins by reviewing the process, ground rules and
basic crisis management concepts. Next, each "player" receives a copy of
the scenario. The leader then walks team members through their expected
responses. Then two or three additional "information updates" are distrib-

uted, followed by a similar discussion of appropriate responses. After the exercise, a short debriefing is conducted. Written comments and feedback are collected later. An evaluation report outlines the strengths observed and improvements needed.

A tabletop exercise is both practice for team members and a test for the plan itself. You will be able to identify the gaps that can result when team members are not fully involved. People whose normal roles are highly specialized will have the chance to recognize the interconnectedness, in emergency response situations, of the various corporate disciplines.

SIMULATION DRILLS

The primary difference between tabletops and simulations is that during simulations, in place of a fixed script and a limited objective, you face a range of occurrences that require team members to improvise. A simulation is a role-playing exercise. It involves two groups—the players, who are the members of your Crisis Management Team being drilled, and the simulators, who are producing the drill and evaluating the players' responses.

The simulators are usually located in a room separate from but near to that of the Crisis Management Team. They are people chosen for their knowledge and expertise in areas appropriate to the simulated incident—such as the site managers.

Drills generally begin at a prearranged start time, with everyone assembled. As a team improves, you might conduct some drills without telling the team members in advance. Intermittent surprise simulations can disrupt busy schedules, but they will ensure your team's readiness. While highly effective, surprise drills require the full support of senior management since they can be disruptive to other priorities.

The players will be operating in the same rooms they would use in a real crisis. A telephone call typically brings the first news of the "crisis." The drill then moves in real time, as simulators introduce additional information to the players via phone, fax, e-mail, pre-recorded mock newscasts and in person. The information revealed to the players about the scenario is dynamic: It changes based on the players' decisions.

In responding, the players *always* contact a member of the simulation team. The backroom simulators in turn have a bank of prepared, predefined moves that they can introduce—events that might actually occur as a crisis unfolds. At the end of the drill, both groups are brought together for a complete debriefing.

A large simulation can involve multiple people, but they don't have to be huge. Participants in their first simulations often report that they thought they were prepared—until they had a chance to put their skills to the test.

It is truly rewarding to see confidence grow among Crisis Management Teams after they have been able to improve their skills. It is through practice that a team becomes a cohesive unit.

ACTIVATION AND NOTIFICATION DRILLS

The third type of drill—which some companies call "code blue emergencies"—is distinct from the others because it is not concerned with a specific risk. Its sole purpose is to streamline the process of assembling your team so that it can quickly get to work. Activation and notification focuses on the processes that have to occur from the moment a company is first made aware of a crisis until all team members are in place.

Some aspects of it are counterintuitive. The first person called is typically not the one with the most decision-making power, but the one who will take longest to arrive at the crisis room. That's because you want as much of the entire team as possible to be present when critical decisions are made.

Some companies call these "code blue" emergencies, so that when the persons on the notification list are called, they understand that it's not a real emergency. Still, team members understand that code blue emergencies take precedence over normal business engagements, just as a real incident would.

DEBRIEFING

No drill should be considered complete until all participants—players and simulators alike—have been debriefed for lessons learned. Debriefing has three objectives:

• Everyone involved should feel increased confidence in their ability to function during a crisis.

- Leaders should learn what parts of the plan need more work. Participants should express these observations, such as "We need more telephones," or "We need somebody who can go to the scene with a laptop specifically loaded for response work," or, "Changing this detail would have made it easier for us to function." You will not only find out how to improve your plan, but will also build ownership on the part of your team members.
- Your people should understand that this is important work, and that the time spent has generated important lessons.

There are four possible conclusions, which you will learn through simulations:

- The team responded well, and the plan proved to be adequate.
- The team responded well, but the plan turned out to be inadequate. You would have discovered that the plan needs revision.
- The team failed to follow the plan. You would have learned that your team members need additional training.
- The team followed the plan, but its response was ineffective. In this case, clearly, the plan needs revision, after which the team will need additional training.

The right simulations can really grab a team's attention. Many players report that they lose track of time.

The next chapter will look at ways to monitor your plans on an ongoing basis, so your company will always be ready.

Quick Use Preparedness Guide

CHAPTER 17: UTILIZING YOUR PLAN

- Have you established a Crisis Management Team?
  - ○ Or several teams, at strategic points and locations?
  - ○ Are team members generally available—or at a minimum, able to stay in constant communication?
  - ○ Are the members able to stay cool under pressure?

- ○ Are they capable of taking decisive action and exercising good judgment without complete information?
- ○ Is your team multidisciplinary?
- ○ Is the mix of members conducive to working as a group?
- ○ Have you trained your team in the content, procedures and specific roles they will plan in a catastrophe?
- Have you designated Crisis Response Leaders at the key levels and locations of your organization?
  - ○ Are these leaders strategically placed, on the ground, at each location where you expect to need a crisis response capability?
  - ○ Are they capable of providing appropriate levels of leadership during a disaster?
- Have you developed a schedule for implementing your plan, taking into account your needs to:
  - ○ Publish crisis preparedness communication pieces?
  - ○ Develop crisis response manuals?
  - ○ Train your team members?
  - ○ Conduct drills?
  - ○ Refine your plans?
- Have you clearly documented your schedule?
- Have you communicated your plans to your people:
  - ○ Through written and oral methods?
  - ○ Through orientation sessions?
  - ○ Through your internal public relations networks?
- Have you conducted thorough drills for the members of your team, including:
  - ○ Tabletop drills?
  - ○ Simulations?
  - ○ Activation and notification drills?
  - ○ Does the scenario incorporate challenges that will test every discipline represented on your team?
  - ○ Are your drill scenarios realistic enough to engage team members and serve as a real preparation?
  - ○ Have you planned debriefings for participants following every drill?
  - ○ Are you ready to incorporate what you learned in the debriefings into revised versions of your plans?

CHAPTER 18

Scrutinizing Yourselves

You have now reviewed the A, E, I, O and U of preparedness planning.

When this plan is implemented, you will feel poised to respond to crisis. And so you should. All of your careful preparation will be fresh in the minds of everyone who will need it, whenever a real incident hits your company.

Except that you have no way of knowing when that might occur.

Neither can you predict what your organization will look like by this time next year—let alone the year after. Who will have left, and who joined? What new operations will you have branched into? In what new locales will your people be working in?

Nor can you imagine today some of the threats that your organizations might face in the future.

So to A, E, I, O and U, you must now add "Sometimes Y": *scrutinizing yourself* in a regular, methodical way.

A Cautionary Tale

The world is not static. Neither is your organization. If you let your preparedness planning stagnate, all the hard work you have done could turn out to be of little use.

CMI once helped a major national retail chain set up a workplace violence response plan and crisis management team. Since that time, though, the retailer has undergone a reorganization. Many people were downsized, while a new CEO brought in a number of managers from his previous organization. Of the ten original members of the team we helped establish, only three are left.

The company has allowed its whole preparedness structure to disintegrate. Does it still have threats and incidents of violence in its stores? Yes—at least as many as ever. But responsibility for its corporate-level response capability has fallen to a single security manager. This company has gone from being a disorganized accident-waiting-to-happen to a methodical, multidisciplinary crisis management team with a plan. Now, because it lacks the habit of regularly scrutinizing itself, it's nearly back where it started.

Preparedness is like muscle tone. If you stop working on it, your ability to respond can atrophy. Conversely, you must remain conditioned, poised and energized for disaster response. You know that the only way to keep your body in shape is to follow a regular regimen of exercise. Likewise, the one way to keep your preparedness planning in shape is through regular drills and rigorous self-scrutiny.

Why Have a Monitoring Process?

Your company surely has management systems in place to regularly monitor each of the functions that are vital to its continuing success, such as sales, accounting or research and development. You must establish another such monitoring system for your crisis preparedness. Your top management must support it. It should kick in at regular intervals—at a minimum, every year. It should have a place in the budget. The people who will be responsible for it must know that they can do a thorough job without feeling pressure either to slight their other responsibilities to the organization, or to skimp on any new controls they identify as necessary.

Nobody in your company would say that it is enough to purchase and operate a fleet of trucks, without ever changing their oil or checking the pressure in their tires. Periodic monitoring and refining is just as essential to preparedness. Monitoring should be presented and understood as part of the preparedness process from day one.

If your preparedness plan is only implemented once—and never revisited and rechecked for ongoing effectiveness—you could be seen as negligent. Your company could be accused of failing to pay attention to evolving hazards. Plaintiff attorneys, government regulators and the public will ask why you didn't remain vigilant, and will compare you unfavorably to companies that did.

Scrutiny Means Revisiting and Revising

The essence of periodically scrutinizing and updating your preparedness plans is twofold.

Revisiting your plan. You will have to walk yourself through all the steps you took to produce the plans you now have in place. That means utilizing all of the analytical and organizational tests we have gone through in the preceding chapters, and applying them to your new situation. Unless the nature of your organization suggests a different frequency, you should thoroughly scrutinize your preparedness at least once each year.

Revising your plan. Then you will have to bring your plans in line with the new information and insights you uncover. Your goal in each round should be to answer the following questions:

- Analyzing foreseeable risks:
  - ○ Do we still face all the risks we used to face?
  - ○ What has changed in our operations or locations that might expose us to new risks?
  - ○ What has changed in the larger economic and political environments that could lead to new risks?
- Evaluating current preparedness:
  - ○ In real incidents, how well were we actually prepared?
    - How closely did our policies and procedures match our needs in real situations? During simulations?
    - How did our Crisis Management Team function under the pressure of real and simulated events?
  - ○ Have changes in personnel created gaps in our preparedness?
    - Have new employees and managers been orientated as to what will be expected of them during crises?
    - Have personnel changes affected the membership and preparedness of our Crisis Management Team?
- Identifying new controls and refinements:
  - ○ Based on the answers to the above questions, what revisions and additions should we make to our preparedness plans?
- Organizing—or, reorganizing—preparedness:

○ How should we incorporate new policies, procedures and people into our preparedness plans?
- Utilizing the revised plan:
  ○ What is the best way to test and refine the revisions?
    ■ What combination of materials, training and drills should we use?

Who Should Be Responsible for Monitoring?

The prudent company charges an individual at the senior level with maintaining its plan's currency. Of course, he or she may delegate the details. But if the initiative for fresh risk analyses or preparedness drills comes from senior management, you can expect these efforts to be taken seriously at every other level.

As with other Management Information Systems, the monitoring methodology for crisis preparedness should be consistent across the company. This way, critical incidents that occur can be clearly defined, so that each location is reporting with the same criteria. Methods for compiling utilized crisis management controls can be provided in a uniform, check-listed, multiple-choice format.

Additionally, your organization can benchmark desired outcomes. Let's say you set a goal to have appointed family representatives to make personal contact with each family of hospitalized or fatally injured employees within four hours after a casualty occurs. You can then measure the actual results.

To get an idea of what else you can measure let's go back to the checklist from Chapter One that denotes "good crisis response":

- Immediate and decisive actions to address the urgent, crisis-related issues and gain control of the situation:
  ○ We can measure how long it takes for the Crisis Management Team to assemble in the Crisis Command Center.
  ○ How quickly are notifications completed?
- Prompt identification of the problems at hand and of the potential for escalation:
  ○ How quickly did the CMT report its compiled list of critical issues to senior management?

- Willingness to assume responsibility, when appropriate, and to "solve" the problems:
  - ○ How quickly did the CMT come up with a solution to the problem and convey it to defined audiences, such as senior management, employees, customers or the media?
- Identification and investigation of root causes:
  - ○ How soon was a team dispatched to identify the cause of the incident?
  - ○ How quickly were initial communications conveyed to defined audiences regarding the investigation of the root cause?
- An effective crisis communications plan that affects all constituents:
  - ○ When did the first notifications or organized communications go out to:
    - Affected employees?
    - Appropriate government regulators?
    - Media?
    - Insurance company?
    - Others?
- Demonstration of compassion and caring in words and actions:
  - ○ How soon was contact with family members of casualties attempted or made?
  - ○ Was every communication to various audiences begun with a statement of heartfelt caring and concern about those who have been affected?
- Accessibility of management to affected individuals and groups including families of casualties, injured and uninjured employees and the media:
  - ○ Did a senior manager make personal contact with the families of serious casualties?
  - ○ Was senior management visible to impacted groups and the media, as appropriate?
- Ongoing steps to make needed short- and long-term changes:
  - ○ Was a debriefing conducted for lessons learned?
  - ○ Were needed changes identified and appropriately reported?
- Minimization of the duration of the crisis:
  - ○ What specific management actions accelerated the recovery process?

- Little or no evidence of lingering outrage or damaged reputation, business disruption, financial impact or harm to individuals:
  - ○ Listed results of feedback coming to management through the family reps, surveys, feedback from crisis consultants working with various affected constituents, occurrence of negative content or spin reported by the media.
  - ○ Were personal stress debriefings provided individually or in a group for managers who responded to the crisis?
- Stability of sales, stock prices and other financial indicators:
  - ○ Maintenance or return of pre-crisis sales within a specified duration?
  - ○ Stock price remains stable or returns to pre-crisis levels within a defined period as compared to the overall market?

To adequately monitor the effectiveness of your crisis management plan, you will need to define actions and outcomes that can be counted or timed. Many of the benchmarked outcomes would require a real crisis, e.g., impact on stock price. Others can be measured in practice drills and simulations. For example, the benchmark may be for the Crisis Management Team members (or their backups) to meet in the Crisis Command Center within thirty minutes of notification. If some of your CMT members live more than thirty minutes from the Crisis Command Center, then you'll need to set up alternative plans for late-hour incidents.

Taking Internal Inventory

Staying prepared means staying current with changes in your organization. Some relevant changes will be obvious—the opening of a new assembly plant in Mexico, perhaps, or the acquisition of another company. Other changes are subtler, but can still have a big effect. For example, if Greenpeace targets one of your competitors for alleged damage to the environment.

Contacting needed persons in the aftermath of a critical incident can be a crisis in itself. It can be especially difficult to contact the spouses of casualties. "Phone numbers are one of the hardest things to keep up to date," reports a CMT leader at a major international company with which CMI has worked. "And in a crunch, you certainly don't want to get sidetracked just because the person you need to reach has a new phone number. We period-ically send out a questionnaire to the people responsible for preparedness at the different levels of the company, with a list of the numbers we need to verify."

Indeed, the inevitable changes in personnel that are always taking place in a large organization can have profound implications for preparedness. Here are some personnel considerations that should be part of your peri-odic monitoring process:

- Regarding new company leadership:
  - ○ Are new people in top management familiar with your pre-paredness plans?
  - ○ Are they committed to preparedness?
  - ○ Have they brought with them a new management team? If so, do those people fully understand and support your plans?
- Regarding new hires:
  - ○ Are your preparedness policies and procedures a routine part of new employee orientation?
  - ○ Do new employees know what will be expected of them in an emergency?
- Regarding promotions and job changes:
  - ○ Have individuals who had specific roles to play in your crisis re-sponse plans been moved to other jobs or given new responsibil-ities that will prevent them from participating?
  - ○ Have their roles been reassigned to other people who are fully briefed and trained in what to do in a crisis?

Bottom line: Someone within your organization needs to take responsi-bility for assuring that your plan is monitored and up-to-date. Just like any other management system, it needs to be a part of someone's job descrip-tion and the resources and authority to make it happen should be pro-vided. Without it, your preparedness will become anemic over time. It is a false sense of security to develop a manual of checklists or provide training to a selected team and expect that you are crisis prepared forever more.

Scrutinizing the Crisis Management Team

Every time you monitor your overall preparedness, you should also scrutinize your CMT.

Examine the group's cohesion. How well has it functioned during drills? How good is the team's leadership? A leader who is too autocratic on the one hand, or too retiring on the other, might have to be replaced. Some companies rotate CMT leaders on a regular basis to ensure fresh approaches.

However you address it, there is no room on your team for halfhearted or incompetent players.

Taking External Inventory

Your organization doesn't exist in a vacuum. When analyzing your current risks, you must consider not only the changes in your own operations but also changing conditions in the world. And similarly, you would do yourselves a disservice to try to keep your preparedness up-to-date without paying attention to what other organizations are doing to avoid and control disasters.

You should continually stay abreast of developments in your industry. How are other companies assessing the risks they face? How are they preparing to cope with those eventualities? Look to industry associations for information on new approaches to preparedness. Other organizations will generally be quite forthcoming about their preparedness plans. They realize, as should you, that a black eye for any member of your industry can be a black eye for the industry as a whole.

Similarly, you should maintain open communication with the governmental regulatory agencies that are charged with responding to crises, such as the Federal Emergency Management Administration, and with local response organizations like fire and police departments and rescue squads, in every place where you maintain operations. Get to know individuals in these organizations. If your company doesn't have a government liaison person or team within your ranks, it might be good to identify connected lobbyists or consultants who can assist during crises and get the attention of government officials.

Ongoing Drills and Debriefings

It is an important challenge to keep simulations fresh each time, and keep the players engaged. After all, there are a limited number of crisis scenarios you can realistically expect to unfold for your organization. But drills can be designed to emphasize different aspects of these scenarios. In one drill you might put emphasis on the speedy analysis of information, while other drills might focus on communicating to the investment community and employees.

It's also important to train for the work that takes place after the immediate response. For example, how do you talk with your customers and employees about any destructive inaccuracies that find their way into the press? What do you do if the community uproar over health and safety does not abate?

It's wise to vary the time frame. Start a crisis simulation with the declaration that the physical destruction has been contained, for instance, or stipulate that the pivotal event took place two days earlier.

One word of caution: In a real crisis, the end of the process tends to have a jagged edge. Team members can easily disband and "not have time" to debrief crisis actions for lessons learned. Also, team members often do not want to dwell on the experience for emotional reasons. Here is the solution: Make it an ironclad policy, with senior management support, that the team *will* debrief within a defined time period after crisis response, and that everyone involved in the crisis response must attend. It may be best to utilize the services of an outside consultant to orchestrate this valuable process, especially if there is also a need to defuse the stress reactions of team members.

Don't forget to update your crisis response manual and procedures to incorporate the lessons—and to make sure the updates are distributed to everyone who needs them. If it fits your culture and the preference of your attorney, it may be wise to assign someone to generate a report that can be used as a training tool.

Just as it may have been difficult to get moving on preparedness in the first place, there is a natural tendency to feel a sense of security once a plan is in place. Get over this illusion. There is no room for complacency or denial. The health and prosperity of your company—and the lives and livelihoods of many are at stake. The job or life you save may be your own.

Quick Use Response Guide

CHAPTER 18: SCRUTINIZING YOURSELVES

- Do you have a plan for monitoring your preparedness at regular intervals, at least annually?
- Is someone in your organization's leadership in charge of self-scrutiny?
- Have you reapplied the A, E, I, O and U of preparedness, asking:
  - ○ Analyzing foreseeable risks:
    - Are the risks you initially considered still threats?
    - What has changed in your operations or locations that might expose you to new risks?
    - What has changed in the larger environments that could lead to new risks?
  - ○ Evaluating current preparedness:
    - If you have experienced recent incidents (or simulations) that required you to go into crisis response mode, how well were you actually prepared?
      - How closely did your policies and procedures match your needs in the real situation?
      - How did your Crisis Management Team function under the pressure of real and simulated events?
    - Have changes in personnel created gaps in your preparedness?
      - Have new employees and managers been oriented as to what will be expected of them during crises?
      - Have personnel changes affected the membership of your Crisis Management Team?
  - ○ Identifying new controls and refinements:
    - Based on the answers to the above questions, what revisions and additions should you make to your preparedness plans?

○ Organizing—reorganizing—preparedness:
  ■ How should you incorporate new policies, and people into your plans?
○ Utilizing the plan:
  ■ What is the best way to test and refine the revisions?
  ■ What combination of training and drills should you use?
• Have you made an internal inventory of your organization to pinpoint changes in:
  ○ Personnel?
  ○ Emergency contact information?
  ○ Places where you operate?
  ○ Activities you are engaged in?
• Have you scrutinized your Crisis Response Team for:
  ○ Efficient operation?
  ○ Effective leadership?
  ○ Appropriate assignments?
  ○ Thorough training?
• Have you kept abreast of developments in preparedness on the part of others in your industry, and emergency response agencies?
• Have you continued to simulate scenarios based on your foreseeable risks?
• Is it a policy that the CMT will debrief for lessons learned after every simulation and crisis response?
• Is it a policy that CMT members will be debriefed to help them personally recover from stressful operations?
• Have you updated your manuals based on what you learned?

CHAPTER 19

A Look into the Future

Often, as a part of our threat-of-violence management services, CMI is asked to make a prediction of violence potential. That's a daunting request, but we know that one of the best predictors of future actions is past behavior. This same concept of "looking forward by looking back" applies in general to the world of corporate crises and the spread of global terrorism.

Catastrophes are more likely now than ever. More people live together in higher densities. Everything is bigger and faster—including methods of mass destruction. However, mass-casualty disasters are not exactly new.

For decades, disgruntled workers have been "going postal," terrorists have hijacked airliners and misfits have slipped poison into consumer products. Carelessness has led to explosions, fires and toxic leaks since the industrial revolution began. Earthquakes, storms and floods are, of course, as old as the planet.

What's changed is only that it is harder to pretend that such things can't happen to our own organizations.

It is human nature to avoid danger, and rightly so. Nobody wants to be at risk. Denial can seem like a way to avoid danger, because it gets the danger off our minds. But the problem with relying on denial as a strategy for responding to risk is that it just plain doesn't work. If we are busy denying risks, we are busy not preparing for them. And excellent leaders are leaders who are prepared.

Preparedness Equals Power

Crisis Management International has discovered firsthand the lessons learned by literally thousands of organizations in crisis. We assisted more than two hundred organizations in New York City during the days after the attacks on the World Trade Center and Pentagon.

Those businesses that were prepared called to inform us that they were putting their plans to work. They reported the actions they were taking and the procedures they were putting into effect, and contacted us only to continue implementing their plans with the on-site support of our consultants.

In sad contrast, those that were unprepared were far slower to make the initial call for assistance. In many cases, when we arrived on the scene, we found that they had taken inappropriate actions. Their responses were significantly less organized, and markedly less effective. Every step was unfamiliar to them—they wanted to discuss each one, when there was so little time to spare. You can imagine the cascading impact of this lack of preparedness on their personal stress levels, the morale of their employees and their ability to get their companies back up and running in the ensuing months.

So What Lies Ahead?

Natural catastrophes and manufacturing disasters have all been around for a long time and will continue. They should not be ignored in lieu of the new terroristic threats throughout the world.

Let's look at where the issue of terrorism may be headed and, on the positive side, the defensive strategies that are evolving. We know that terrorism can affect all of us. And even though it's frightening to contemplate, we must examine the ways in which terrorism is mutating.

Leverage. Terrorists understand, just as well as businesspeople, the power of leveraging—applying limited resources to strategic points to create enormous effects. With a few airplane tickets and some box cutters, the terrorists of September 11, 2001, exacted a catastrophic price from the world. Soon after, for the price of a few microbes, a stamp and an envelope, anthrax terrorists were able to close down American office buildings for weeks at a time.

The good news is that companies and government entities also understand how to leverage. Inexpensive protections are emerging. It's now harder for a hijacker to commandeer an airplane. Relatively inexpensive enhancements of flight deck doors, and the readiness of passengers to fight anyone trying to overtake an airplane, make a repeat performance much more difficult. You, too, can utilize the concept of leverage in your organization to get the most payoff for your preparedness efforts.

Copycats. We know from history that individual and group copycats will emerge and jump on the terrorism bandwagon.

But corporations and the government are banding together to come up with controls to combat terrorism. Just as terrorists copy each other, your company can benchmark and study the methods and lessons learned from other organizations. In today's less secure environment, you owe it to yourselves to pay attention to the best practices in prevention, preparedness and response. Those who ignore them open themselves up to charges of negligence.

New methods and new targets. Terrorism is becoming more insidious. New methods of concern include the NBC's (nuclear, biological and chemical). As we look at terrorist acts perpetrated upon America, we realize the targets are at the center of our democratic power and strength. The heart of the world's financial system was attacked twice at the World Trade Center. The nation's military brainpower was attacked at the Pentagon. Institutions in our free enterprise system, corporations, schools, religious establishments, public works facilities and government properties are all potential targets.

The good news is that new methods of defense and response are surfacing. The need for advanced screening, security and monitoring will continue to make sophisticated equipment and services available to every organization.

Progressive severity. As soon as the bar is reset to a new height, people strive to jump over it. This holds true as well in the world of terrorism. America progressively went from the Unabomber, to the 1993 World Trade Center bombing, to the 1995 Oklahoma City bombing to the attacks in 2001. Each was more severe than the ones before. We hate to think about the possibility of nuclear power plants being attacked and making areas the size of New York State uninhabitable. But we have evidence that terrorists are considering it. Possibly the greatest damage done by the September 11, 2001, terrorism was the "threshold damage"—the raising of the bar for future incidents.

It is imperative that we in the corporate world begin to think the unthinkable: If you are located in a major city near a nuclear facility, for example, what would you do if the area became radioactive, so no one could inhabit it for decades? We owe it to ourselves to think outside the "severity box." The terrorists do it, and so must we.

The Expectation of Preparedness

People everywhere have now watched the way large-scale disasters unfold. They have seen the ways in which organizations were, and were not, prepared. So the public and your workers expect you to protect them. Rightly or wrongly, your response will be compared to that of other entities. Legions of regulators, reporters and plaintiff attorneys arise to "help" the public make such judgments.

As never before, employees, investors and others associated with your organization expect you to be prepared.

Facing the Uncertain Future with Care and Calm

If you were to go to a therapist because you felt overwhelmed, you might hear advice like this: "You're entitled to feel overwhelmed. Life truly is messy. And scary. The things coming at you are unpredictable. Your own reactions can be contradictory and confusing. Nothing I can tell you, and nothing you can do, can make life logical, or simple, or certain, or completely safe. All you can do is to examine yourself, clarify your intentions, pay attention, and do your best. If you do those things, you won't feel so overwhelmed. You may even have a good time."

So take a deep breath, find the resolve to prepare yourself, and go on living life to the fullest in this uncontrollable world. Paradoxically, people and organizations with the greatest sense of peace are those who have openly examined their risks, and prepared for them as well as they can.

Now is the time to increase your vigilance. Establish a crisis planning committee. Review your preparedness plans. Identify your new foreseeable risks. Address the expectations of your people, and demonstrate to them that you are prepared. Effectively work to prevent incidents from occurring if at all humanly possible. Get experienced crisis consultants from all the appropriate disciplines on retainer. And be ready to respond to the business *and* human needs should you be next to have tragedy knock on your door.

I hope you will be lucky enough to be spared disaster. But if you are not, I trust this book will help you prepare and respond with strength and grace.

If we protect even one person from harm, then our efforts are well worth it.

Quick Use Preparedness Guide

CHAPTER 19: A LOOK INTO THE FUTURE

The single greatest obstacle to crisis preparedness is in not getting started. It is not what you read or understand in this book that is useful. It is only what you take and use that counts. Make a commitment to start your preparedness now.

CHAPTER 20

Incident Checklists

This chapter provides you with guidelines and considerations for a variety of catastrophic incidents that could affect your organization. These lists are designed to supplement the more generic response guidelines provided previously in the first ten chapters. The checklists are organized into two sections: Immediate Actions and Unique Considerations.

These checklists are not meant to be exhaustive. They are simply provided as guidelines to get you started in the right direction when a catastrophic incident occurs. The first half of the book offers additional actions.

It is recommended that you and your Crisis Planning Committee or Crisis Management Team review these guidelines in detail. Additions and deletions should be customized to fit your corporate culture. Manuals can be developed with tabs for quick reference. A handheld electronic version and a Web-based software version is also suggested for rapid access at any time.

These guidelines assume that 911 has been contacted and the "proverbial" fire alarm has been sounded. Items are not listed in priority order.

No checklist is complete because the decisions made and actions taken are a result of the progression of emerging issues. It is your responsibility to determine the order of listed actions to take and which to omit, according to the fact pattern of the incident when you first become involved.

Accidental Deaths

IMMEDIATE ACTION STEPS

❑ Have onlookers move away from the area where the deceased persons are located.
❑ Ensure that no one else has been injured.
❑ Notify immediate family members.
❑ Assume all blood and body fluids are infectious.
❑ *Do not* remove/move the body unless absolutely necessary.
❑ Cover the body to shield it from onlookers.
❑ Keep people away from any areas that may be dangerous.
❑ Get names, addresses and phone numbers of witnesses.
❑ *Do not* remove any evidence that could affect the investigation.
❑ *Do not* ask your own employees to clean up any gruesome areas. Hire an outside janitorial service for this distressing job.
❑ Assure that every object subjected to body fluids is doused with a one-part bleach to ten-parts water solution.

UNIQUE CONSIDERATIONS

○ Determine if the workplace or work area will be closed/shut down following the incident.
○ Arrange for employees who witnessed the incident or its aftermath to receive professional crisis mental health assistance.
○ If the dead include outsiders, like customers, contractors, etc., a determination will need to be made whether or not to assign family representatives.
○ If the decedent is an employee, OSHA will investigate. Prepare employees to fully cooperate with the investigation.
○ If a crime is suspected, ask employees not to talk about the incident until law enforcement has interviewed each witness.
○ Be aware of anyone who is blamed or scapegoated. They can be severely distressed or even targets of hostility.
○ Expect questions about safety and fears of recurrence.
○ Funeral attendance policy and procedures will need to be communicated.

Aircraft Crash

IMMEDIATE ACTION STEPS

❑ If a business jet, verify that it is your jet through positive identification of the tail of the plane.
❑ Obtain the names of the passengers on the manifest.
❑ Verify fatalities vs. injuries.
❑ Notify immediate family members.
❑ Confirm the present location of wreckage.
❑ Locate hospitals where victims were sent.
❑ Collect ongoing updates on injured requiring hospital treatment.
❑ Establish a place where family members can congregate.

UNIQUE CONSIDERATIONS

○ Send family representatives to families of casualties.
○ Consider possible criminal activity or sabotage.
○ Anticipate the involvement of NTSB and FAA in the investigation.
○ Anticipate Environmental Protection Agency (EPA) involvement if there is a spill of jet fuel.
○ If a serious crash involves senior executives, anticipate a reaction from the investment community.
○ Provide travel accommodations for family members who will want to travel to remote locations to be with their hospitalized loved ones.
○ Family representatives may need to go to the remote location of the crash site.
○ Consider whether family representatives should accompany family members en route to the site or meet them there.
○ Ensure that an adequate community outreach program is initiated, if locals on the ground were affected.

Biochemical Exposure

IMMEDIATE ACTION STEPS

❑ Isolate the suspicious materials in a certified biohazard security bag (re-sealable plastic bags can be used as long as the items are double-bagged).

❑ Immediately shut off the ventilation system to slow its spread.

❑ Close and secure all doors in the area.

❑ Contact local law enforcement and/or the FBI.

❑ Exposed individuals should wash their hands quickly and thoroughly with a biochemical-certified antibacterial disinfectant.

❑ Potentially exposed individuals should be advised not to touch eyes, face, mouth, eyes or other body parts until they have washed their hands.

❑ Remove contaminated clothing and place in large resealable bags.

❑ Notify all employees, especially those who receive or handle incoming packages, mail or similar substances to the contaminant.

❑ Individuals who have apparently been exposed should be separated from other employees and assigned to stay in a specific area. This area should be clearly identified to prevent non-exposed employees from entering if possible.

❑ Potentially exposed individuals should be advised not to leave the area.

❑ Immediately retrace the route of the package to identify additional contaminated items and areas, such as:
   ○ Desktops
   ○ Mail bins
   ○ Other mail delivered at the same time as the package
   ○ Personal items used by exposed individuals
   ○ Items used by the exposed individuals (pens, paper, telephone, chair, phone book, pager, computer keyboard, etc.)
   ○ Individuals who may have come in contact with the suspicious substance, along with their contact information

❑ List all exposed items and notify law enforcement.

⇨

UNIQUE CONSIDERATIONS

○ Be sure to protect all suspicious package pieces, outside paper, stamps, tape and mailing labels, etc.

○ Provide education and information through a medical specialist in bio-hazards.

○ Log the date and time of delivery along with the delivery personnel's name and company.

○ Notify any delivery services whose personnel also have been exposed.

○ The affected area should remain roped or taped off until thoroughly evaluated and/or decontaminated.

○ Your building may be closed off for several days or weeks. Make plans to continue business in an alternate location.

Chemical/Toxic Exposure

IMMEDIATE ACTION STEPS

Chemicals

❑ Block off and guard the spill.
❑ Ventilate or seal off the area, as appropriate.
❑ Call in a specialist in chemical spills, as needed.

Toxic Exposure

❑ Evaluate the risk of further exposure and consider evacuation.
❑ If the worksite is to be evacuated, the evacuation route should be up-wind.
❑ Identify the source of the fumes, and safely stop them if you can.
❑ Secure the exposed area. Tape windows and doors to contain fumes, if necessary.
❑ Shut off all heating, cooling and ventilation systems.
❑ If in a cafeteria, determine if any food may have been contaminated.
❑ Assign an individual(s) to keep people out of the exposed area. If necessary, have someone guard the driveways to prevent people from entering the property.
❑ Account for all employees. Get affected visitor names, if appropriate.
❑ Contact neighboring businesses and community representatives if exposure risk exists.
❑ Arrange expert clean up/repair, as needed.

UNIQUE CONSIDERATIONS

○ Seek specialty medical advice and treatment.
○ Consider providing medical education/Q & A for staff, family members and others regarding the effects of the specific exposure.
○ Prepare for lingering concerns over the potential long-term effects of exposure.
○ Anticipate the involvement of the Environmental Protection Agency, OSHA and other regulators. Determine their needs and probable actions.

Civil Unrest

IMMEDIATE ACTION STEPS

❏ Coordinate corporate response with the appropriate embassies, security advisors, law enforcement and government agencies.
❏ Account for all employees and their family members.
❏ Many times it is better for employees and families to stay put behind closed doors.
❏ If evacuation is chosen:
   ○ Premises only or leave the country?
   ○ Employees should evacuate to what location(s)?
❏ Organize and facilitate ongoing communications with employees and family members.
❏ Establish a redundant communications source for backup, in case the primary communications source is disabled or monitored.
❏ Coordinate employee/family needs during emergency evacuation.
❏ Communicators stay in close contact with embassies, law enforcement and government agencies for approval of any statements to the public.
❏ Implement board-up procedures and secure all facility openings if building is evacuated.

UNIQUE CONSIDERATIONS

○ Identify all prescription medication needs of employees and family members, so they are not separated from their medication for long.
○ Determine the safety hazards that may occur for communities and re-turning employees if a worksite is left unmanned over time.
○ Identify expatriates' homeland family members and provide ongoing communications to them.
○ Assign family representatives to homeland family-members.
○ Anticipate re-entry issues for returning ex-patriots.

Earthquakes

IMMEDIATE ACTION STEPS

❑ Assess any significant injuries or damage to the facilities.

❑ Check for structural damage, gas leaks and electrical hazards. If needed, shut off the gas or electrical supply source.

❑ If evacuation becomes necessary, exit the building away from windows, shelves and heavy objects.

❑ Move employees to pre-designated areas well away from the building, exterior windows and vulnerable objects, e.g., parking-lot light poles.

❑ Account for everyone. Check for those who may have been left behind.

❑ Identify and prioritize those in need of medical attention.

❑ Do not move any seriously injured individual(s) unless doing so is absolutely necessary.

❑ Clear driveways of debris, to allow emergency vehicles in and out.

❑ Anticipate that emergency medical services may be overwhelmed and streets impassable. If appropriate, consider taking injured persons to the hospital.

❑ Verify that hospitals are operational. Determine alternative locations for medical care, if hospitals and other treatment facilities are full or inoperable.

❑ Employees will be extremely concerned about their loved ones in the affected area. Assist them with communications ASAP, via telephone, cell phone, transportation, etc.

❑ Enlist the contractors and suppliers to assist with repairs to the work facility. Contract with them immediately, before they become overwhelmed with other requests.

❑ Quickly secure providers to assist employees with home repairs, motel rooms, rental cars and other commodities that may be in high demand.

UNIQUE CONSIDERATIONS

○ Provide security measures to prevent looting.

○ Do not let anyone go back into the building unless you know its structure is sound.

○ Organize assistance for employee disaster victims whose houses were destroyed, with food, shelter, cash, day care, transportation, etc.   ⇨

○ Anticipate that some employees may need shelter if either they cannot reach their homes or their homes were destroyed.

○ Anticipate requests for leave to address home repairs and meet insurance adjusters, as well as an increase in stress-related absences.

○ Ensure ongoing communications to and from employees, especially those who have to protect and repair their property.

○ Organize less-affected employees to assist in humanitarian efforts.

○ Provide armed guards if cash is provided to employees or if supplies provided to employees are in high demand locally.

○ Retrieve and secure important records.

Explosion/Fire

IMMEDIATE ACTION STEPS

❑ Move evacuated people away from the building and areas where there could be a secondary explosion.

❑ If a bomb is suspected, keep employees away from vehicles, Dumpsters, etc., where additional bombs could be planted.

❑ Instruct everyone to shut down the following electronic equipment, which could inadvertently trigger a bomb that uses a remote sensor:
  • Walkie-talkies
  • Cellular phones
  • Two-way radios
  • All other wireless two-way communication devices

❑ Clear a path for emergency vehicles to enter and exit the premises.

❑ Make sure all building doors are closed. Do not allow anyone to enter a burning building.

❑ Provide firefighters with a blueprint of the building.

❑ If arson or other crime is suspected, do not move any articles, and protect the incident site.

❑ Establish a receiving area for arriving family members.

❑ If the incident exposes the neighboring community, contact local officials.

UNIQUE CONSIDERATIONS

○ Have someone locate the nearest fire hydrant prior to the arrival of firefighters.

○ Conduct a phone tree or other method to assess the status of every employee. Ask them to report to a designated location the next day for a management-led briefing meeting (off-site, if necessary).

○ Once the fire is out:
  • Beware of electrical/water and structural hazards
  • Elevate valuables off the floor to reduce water damage

○ Be prepared to discuss the (real or perceived) effects of burns or toxic exposures publicly, enlisting a recognized burn unit physician and a toxic exposure specialist.

Flood

IMMEDIATE ACTION STEPS

If a flood is detected in vicinity:

❏ Begin sandbagging operations.
❏ Obtain water contamination procedures from local officials.
❏ Make sure that valuables are elevated to a level higher than the forecasted flood level.
❏ Cancel all shipments, as appropriate.
❏ Turn off electrical power, when appropriate.
❏ Inform people to stay away from dangerous areas, e.g., contaminated floodwaters, unstable structures, electrical hazards, etc.
❏ Provide security measures to prevent looting.
❏ Anticipate and make arrangements for employees who may need shelter if they cannot reach their homes or if homes were destroyed.

If there is property damage as a result of the flood:

❏ Enter the building with caution. Snakes and other animals may have entered the building. Electrical hazards may exist. Provide protective equipment.
❏ Ensure that the electrical service is safe before turning on the power.
❏ Inspect the building to assess structural damage

UNIQUE CONSIDERATIONS

○ Anticipate and arrange for the supplies and equipment you'll need to reopen the facility.
○ Employees who come in contact with floodwaters may need tetanus shots.
○ Consider organizing assistance for the employees whose homes have suffered severe damage.

Kidnap and Ransom

IMMEDIATE ACTION STEPS

❏ Notify your kidnap and ransom insurer and/or hostage negotiation firm.

❏ Set up a kidnap response command center, with a security plan that can ensure the safety of crisis-team members, communicators, etc.

❏ Establish a method to record phone calls.

❏ Notify kidnapped victims' families.
  ○ Be cautious: Remember the possibility of a false kidnapping notification.

❏ Obtain current medical history on hostages, including prescription drug information and dates of inoculations.

❏ Begin a log of all events.

❏ Obtain statements from witnesses (in conjunction with law enforcement):
  ○ Location of the kidnapping
  ○ Vehicle used by kidnappers
  ○ Weapons used by kidnappers
  ○ Any other identifying information available about the kidnappers
  ○ Any ransom note or communication from the kidnappers
  ○ Any other eyewitnesses to the kidnapping

❏ Determine if there are other potential targets for kidnapping.

❏ Identify hostages from other companies, if any, and coordinate your response with their management team.

UNIQUE CONSIDERATIONS

○ Locate photographs of the hostages for the authorities.

○ Provide a hair sample sealed in an airtight container for possible DNA matching (obtained from the victims' hairbrushes, if needed).

○ Identify the specific blood types of hostages.

○ Maintain law enforcement liaisons and embassy liaisons for two-way communications and information.

○ Provide the full names, ages and physical, medical and emotional conditions of hostages to authorities/negotiators.

⇨

○ Monitor domestic and foreign media and press reports related to the kidnapping.
○ Protect families from media encroachments.
○ Assign family representatives to family members of hostages.
○ Provide crisis mental health assistance for family members who will need assistance over the long haul.
○ Research information on the terrorist groups who are active in the area.
○ Provide available information to family members. Explain reasons for confidentialities by negotiators/law enforcement.
○ Explain to family members how negotiations work.
○ Give family members information about the nature of the kidnappers, if known.
○ Prepare for the psychological needs of hostages upon release.
○ Plan the actions you will need to take, in the event that the hostages are killed.

Shooting

IMMEDIATE ACTION STEPS

❑ Assess if the incident presents a continuing danger.

❑ Obtain the physical description of the attacker, including any distinguishing characteristics.

❑ Have someone remain on the line with a 911 operator if the situation is ongoing.

❑ Immediately dispatch company representatives to provide or assist law enforcement with serious injury/death notification(s).

❑ Thoroughly search the property and surrounding areas for any employees who may still be in hiding.

❑ Law enforcement officers may give early media statements. Coordinate your messages with theirs.

UNIQUE CONSIDERATIONS

○ Identify witnesses for law enforcement investigation.

○ Protect the crime scene and weapon(s) from any contamination that could obstruct law enforcement investigation.

○ Call for external cleanup and repair services, as needed. Do not allow any on-site employees to clean up a bloody crime scene. Beware of blood-borne hazards.

○ Arrange for security personnel to protect victims at the hospital, especially if further violence is possible.

○ Identify the location of victims in the hospitals—they may be admitted under an alias (standard procedure for gunshot victims).

○ Determine what to do with the desk/work area of fatally injured employee(s).

Dear Reader: Please feel free to contact me at:
Crisis Management International, Inc.
CMI@cmiatl.com
1-800-274-7470
1-800-CRISIS-(0)

or check out our website:
www.cmiatl.com

Permission granted to use the quote from Captain Al Haynes on Flight 232 from the audio narrative *Teamwork in Crisis: The Miracle of Flight 232* © CRM Learning 2001; Chris Nelson of Target granted permission to use the text describing Target's actions regarding Safeness; James Kreindler (partner in the law firm Kreindler and Kreindler, who is quoted about his work in the Pan Am 103 plaintiffs' suit); Jack Cox granted permission to use the information from Liberty Mutual. Permission granted to use the study "The Impact of Catastrophes on Shareholder Value" published by Templeton College of Oxford; Joy Sever, Director of Reputation Research at the Reputation Institute, granted permission to report on how crises affect companies.

"The Impact of Catastrophes on Shareholder Value"
Rory F. Knight & Debroah J. Pretty
A Research Report Sponsored by Sedgwick Group Order by
fax, phone, email or post (payment required with order):
Publication Sales, Accounts Department, Templeton College
University of Oxford, Oxford, OX1 5NY
Fax +44(0) 1865 422501   Tel +44 (0) 1865 422779
Email your credit card order to
publications@templeton.ox.ac.uk